DOD KNOWS
(The Jimmy Book)

By

David Thurman

Dedication: To those whose love becomes

a heritage for generations to come

Printed by CreateSpace, an Amazon.com Company

Available on Amazon.com and other online stores

© 2006, 2018 W. David Thurman

THE CALL Logo and cover contribution by Mary Thurman

All rights reserved. No part of this book may be reproduced in any form without the express written consent of the author.

Author's Note: The stories in this book are true life events. The telling of the stories is a wonderful part of community, and is framed by perception, memory, and relationship. Some of the names of persons described have been changed to protect their privacy.

DOD KNOWS

PROLOGUE
1. IN AND OUT 3
2. ACCEPTANCE . . . 9
3. HUBBA HUBBA . . . 19
4. ONE TRACK 26
5. MY HOUSE FIRST . . . 32
6. DILIGENCE IN LEARNING . . 38
7. CLEAN BATHE . . . 49
8. NO ME FALL DOWN . . . 57
9. FELLA AND LADY . . . 66
10. 1-2-3-4-5 73
11. LIKE SHARON BEST . . 81
12. TUTDOWN TAUBURN! . . 89
13. HEY FWIEND! . . . 97
14. MARCH IN WEDDING . . 104
15. NOW YOU LEARN! . . . 113
16. HARD UNNERTAN . . . 120
17. NO ME FUTH TOMPAIN . . 128
18. INITIATION . . . 135
19. BIG TURKEY DAY . . . 144
20. MEME 151
21. THE UNCLES . . . 156
22. OL' BALD HEAD . . . 163
23. BABY SISTER . . . 171
24. DOD KNOWS . . . 178
25. HARD AS BWICK . . . 184
26. HIS BIRTHDAY . . . 191
27. JUBILEE 200
POSTLOGUE

PROLOGUE

We were sitting at the breakfast table in Alabama at the house of my Grandmother ("Meme") and Grandaddy ("Papa"). This was one of my favorite places and one of my favorite times. Grandmother was famous for her Alabama breakfasts - eggs, bacon, sausage, grits, made from scratch biscuits with homemade fig and pear preserves, and wild Muscadine grape jelly. We called it a "Meme breakfast," and it appeared on the table daily.

We ate our fill, relishing Grandmother's good "down home" cooking. After the meal, we sat and talked - Grandmother, Grandaddy, Jimmy and my family. The conversation meandered, but eventually it came around to one of our favorite topics - Jimmy. Grandmother told a few stories about Jimmy. Some of the stories were funny and we laughed. A couple of the stories were poignant and we felt their meaning as she told them.

After awhile, Grandaddy turned and focused on Jimmy. With a tone of intentional certainty, he said, "Jimmy is more valuable to us than anything in the world."

I looked at Jimmy. Jimmy just sat there.

Now Jimmy was a talker. He didn't just listen and respond. Jimmy initiated conversation. Conversation confirmed relationship and Jimmy was a relational person. He didn't miss many opportunities to talk.

But on this occasion, Jimmy didn't respond. As I looked into Jimmy's eyes though, I could see that he felt the full impact of that statement. He did not have the look of a man that had just been flattered - although a compliment was clearly intended. Jimmy had the look of a man that was accepted - a person who fully belonged. Jimmy realized exactly what was being said.

Grandaddy continued, "We wouldn't trade Jimmy for all the money in the world." Jimmy sat there and never said a word. He didn't need to say anything. He knew where he stood.

CHAPTER ONE
IN AND OUT

Grandmother (also affectionately known as "Meme") used to say:

When Jimmy came to live with us, he was hard to handle. He was almost six years old. He couldn't feed himself, he couldn't dress himself, and you could barely understand anything that he said.

His father had left his family. His mother could not take care of him. She had to work, and caring for Jimmy was a 24 hour a day job. His grandmother tried to care for him, but she could not control him. He was wild, and he ran away a number of times. He would run to the candy store, grab a handful of candy, and run off with it. His grandmother began locking the door of her apartment in order to keep him from running away. He was cooped up inside all day long - day after day after day.

I knew his history and I watched him closely during his first day at our house. Jimmy acted like a little boy who had been locked in a cage. He basically did one thing. He went to the front door and stood in front of it. He then opened it, went through it, and stood outside for a few minutes. Then he opened the front door and stepped back inside. In and out. In and out. He spent the whole day just going in and out. The idea that he could actually go through a door to the outside world was a strange and wonderful concept for him.

JAMES CARLTON STUCKEY, JR. was born on October 22, 1949. He was a Downs Syndrome child. At that time, Downs Syndrome children were called "mentally retarded" - or simply "Mongoloid."

Jimmy's parents were never a part of his life. Jimmy's father rejected him from birth.

Jimmy's mother probably tried to care for Jimmy, but she gave him up when he was a baby. Jimmy's paternal grandmother, Lena Stuckey (known as Ma'maw), became his primary care giver. Ma'maw Stuckey had problems controlling Jimmy.

Uncle David says:

When Jimmy was living with his grandmother, he would run away a lot. Sometimes, the police would find him out alone and wandering. They had no way of communicating with Jimmy and often did not know who he was or where he belonged.

I babysat for Jimmy one time when I was twelve. He was about five years old. I left the front door unlocked, and Jimmy ran out of the house like a flash. I tell you what, he was fast. I was twice as big as he was and it took me two blocks to catch that guy.

The Martin family was introduced to Jimmy through a mutual friend, Jimmy Glenn. Mr. Glenn knew Jimmy's grandmother, Ma'maw Stuckey. She and Jimmy attended a small church group in Greenville, Alabama that the Martin's sometimes visited.

Ma'maw Stuckey tried to care for Jimmy, but it was a struggle. The final straw occurred when Jimmy threw some keys and hit her in the eye. Jimmy certainly did not intend to hurt his grandmother. Thankfully, the eye injury was not serious or permanent. It scared Ma'maw though, and she realized that Jimmy was simply too much for her to handle.

Grandmother used to say:

Even though Jimmy was almost six years old when he came to us, he was still eating baby food. For the first few weeks, I had to feed him baby food because that is all he knew how to eat. After a few days of seeing the rest of the children eat regular food, Jimmy

began to want to eat that food as well. It wasn't long before he was eating normal food like everybody else.

Grandaddy used to say:

When Jimmy came to us, the experts said that he would be severely handicapped. He wouldn't be able to ride a bike or write his name. What concerned us most though is that they said he probably would not live past the age of 12. People with Jimmy's condition have very large tongues. The doctors told us that some retarded children suffocated in their sleep because their tongue blocked their breathing passages. We always tried to keep an eye on Jimmy during his sleep, especially when he was younger.

Jimmy did have an extremely large tongue. When he stuck it out of his mouth, it looked like a cow's tongue. Jimmy could stick his tongue out of his mouth and touch the tip of his nose with it. This display was an endless source of amusement for us children, and Jimmy was more than happy to oblige us.

"Jimmy!" we often asked. "Please stick your tongue out and touch your nose."

Jimmy smiled. His large tongue emerged like a pink eel from his cavernous mouth. We laughed with glee. Jimmy wagged his tongue side to side for extra effect. He giggled and snorted at his own antics. He usually had to pull his tongue back in so he didn't choke on his own laughter. Then, out came the tongue again.

After a few aborted attempts, Jimmy curled his tongue upward. As his tongue neared his nose, Jimmy's eyes crossed making a peculiar face. We children cheered and Jimmy touched the tip of his nose with ease. He then laughed at us as we stuck out our tongues and tried to touch our noses. We could not even touch our nose, much less the tip of it.

Watching Jimmy eat was another interesting display - if you could stand it. Jimmy enjoyed his food, and he showed it. His tongue half surrounded, and half crushed his food. Jimmy usually chewed with his mouth open. The inside of his mouth looked like a food processing plant. Jimmy slurped, smacked and swallowed, then said *"Mmm! Duud meal!"* (good meal).

Jimmy came to stay with the Martin family in Montgomery, Alabama in September of 1955. Grandaddy and Grandmother Martin had nine children of their own. There were two girls - Rachel (my mother) and Aunt Rebecca, and seven boys - Uncles Mark, Stephen, David, Timothy, Daniel, Andy, and Thomas. When Jimmy came, eight of those children were still at home.

Grandmother used to say:

We had a visitor from our church who came to see us one afternoon. He and Papa sat down on the front porch to play a game of checkers and talk. As they were playing, children started walking by and going in and out - first one child, and then another.

The visitor watched all these children for a while and then asked, "Where do all these children come from?"

Papa said, "They're my children."

The visitor was a little surprised. "All of them?"

Papa said, "Yes. All of them."

The visitor pondered for a minute. Then he asked, "Why did you have all these children, Tom?"

Papa chuckled and then said, "Well, you know the Bible says to be fruitful and multiply, and to replenish the earth."

The visitor paused and said, "Well, you're right. The Bible does say that. But it doesn't say that you're supposed to do it all by yourself!"

Grandmother and Grandaddy had a large family to support and they had very little money. At the time Jimmy came to stay with them, they lived in a rented farm house which had three bedrooms and one bathroom. Grandaddy and Grandmother were married in Texas in the middle of the Great Depression. They had to borrow the money to pay for their marriage license. They managed to scratch out a living during those difficult years.

Grandmother used to say:

Not long after we got married, a neighbor knocked on our door one morning. Their child needed 5 cents for milk money for school. The neighbors only had 2 cents in the house, and came to ask us for a nickel. We looked, but Papa and I didn't have any money either - not even a nickel. We were just about to give up when I remembered that I had saved a few pennies in my sewing drawer. I looked in my sewing drawer and I had 4 pennies - enough to make the milk money. On that particular day, between our two families we had total cash of 6 cents. Those were some hard times, but we had each other.

I was once told that Grandaddy never made more than $10,000.00 dollars in any year of his life. Notwithstanding the large family, the crowded house and the financial struggles, Grandaddy and Grandmother made a decision to receive a special needs child into their home. When Ma'maw Stuckey realized she could not care for Jimmy in 1955, the State of Alabama was prepared to institutionalize him. Grandaddy actually went and visited the state facility into which Jimmy would have been placed. He found the conditions deplorable.

Grandmother used to say:

When Jimmy came to live with us, we didn't know how or even if we could handle it. We didn't have much money and we had such a large family. We obviously didn't have any space for him in the

house. But someone had to do it. Either we were going to take him or he was going to go to the state. We felt that we simply had to take him into our home.

Looking back, the decision to accept Jimmy was not a responsible decision. Grandmother and Grandaddy had nine other children, no money, no room and no outside assistance. It was a mystery to many people. What caused the Martins to bring an undisciplined, "mentally retarded" child like Jimmy into their home?

CHAPTER TWO
ACCEPTANCE

Grandmother used to say:

When Jimmy was little, the other boys in the family didn't want Jimmy to play games with them. He didn't understand the rules, he didn't understand how to play, and he didn't understand the purpose of the game. They felt that he would only get in the way and mess up the game. When the other boys were playing a game outside, Jimmy would go out to see them. But he would stand alone on the side and watch them play.

One day though, the boys wanted to play a football game. The teams were not even and they needed one more person to play. They could not find anyone else, so some one finally suggested that they let Jimmy play with them. They put Jimmy on one of the teams.

A few hours later the boys came back into the house. They were laughing and hooting and hollering. They were almost rolling in the floor. They said "That is the most fun that we have ever had! When Jimmy plays, nobody knows what Jimmy is going to do and nobody knows what is going to happen next. That is the funniest thing we have ever seen!"

From that point on, when the boys played football, Jimmy was asked to play with them every time. The boys insisted on it.

Jimmy loved to play football. Actually, he loved to play any game. Jimmy was intensely competitive, and he loved the revelry of team events.

I didn't see that first football game with Jimmy. I was too young to have seen it. Jimmy was ten years older than I. While growing up though, I observed and participated in hundreds of football games with Jimmy.

When you played football with Jimmy, you learned two important lessons. You particularly learned these lessons if you were young and small like me. The first lesson was: Rules are important. You quickly realized that rules are important because when you played football with Jimmy - there were none.

Jimmy did not understand many rules about football, and during the excitement of the game, he tended to forget what few rules he did know. No one knew what Jimmy was going to do at any moment. Every play was unpredictable. The result was uproarious bedlam, even when we were older.

In a typical football game with Jimmy, Jimmy insisted that he be the person to kickoff to the other team. Jimmy had an appreciation for the importance of the kicking game, and he loved to kick the ball. Jimmy's kickoffs were almost always punts. Jimmy could kick the ball from the ground, but he rarely had a teammate (including me) who was brave enough to kneel down and hold the ball for Jimmy while he ran up and took a swipe at the ball with his foot.

At the beginning of a football game, Jimmy took the ball to punt it. He didn't just drop the ball on his foot. He tossed the ball up in the air (often higher than his head), and then lashed at it with his right leg. I say "lashed" because Jimmy didn't play sports lackadaisically. Jimmy did not hold anything back. He gave 100% effort every time and all the time. Unfortunately, on this occasion, he missed the ball with his right foot, his left foot slipped, and he landed on his rear end. When he landed, Jimmy's right leg was sticking straight up in the air, still fully extended. Jimmy kind of grunted and rolled over.

I heard snickers from the other players on the field. I tried to control my own amusement as I went over to help Jimmy up.

"Jimmy, are you okay?" I asked.

"*Yeah be aw wight*" he said.

Jimmy picked up the ball as if nothing unusual had happened and we lined up to kickoff again. Jimmy threw the ball up and this time he made partial contact with the ball. The ball went off on a diagonal angle end over end, and we ran after it. Jimmy, who had stopped to admire his kick, tailed behind us. A player on the other team, Stephen, fielded the ball and ran for about 10 yards before we tagged him. We stopped because the play was over.

Over, that is, for every one but Jimmy. Jimmy didn't necessarily understand the concept of the end of a play. Jimmy did understand that Stephen had the ball and that possession of the ball was an important thing. About three seconds after we tagged Stephen and stopped, Jimmy came running through the group and barreled into Stephen.

Stephen exclaimed "Hey!" as he crashed to the ground. The rest of us said "Whoa, Jimmy! Stop! The play is over!" Jimmy was trying to wrestle the ball from Stephen. We eventually pulled Jimmy off of Stephen. We were laughing as we did so, although Stephen didn't act as if he found much humor in the matter as he scraped himself up off the ground.

The teams huddled. "Jimmy," I said, "you rush the quarterback. You try to get the man with the ball. Do you understand?"

Jimmy shook his head affirmatively and said "*Yeth*."

The two teams lined up at the line of scrimmage. I put Jimmy in front of the center and whispered a reminder. "Jimmy, get the man with the ball."

Jimmy didn't necessarily understand the concept of the line of scrimmage. The opposing center prepared to hike the ball to the quarterback. While the center still held the ball, however, Jimmy jumped on the ball as if it were a fumble, landing on the center's arm in the process. Jimmy and the center tumbled to the ground with Jimmy tugging for the ball with all he had.

"Wait, Jimmy, wait!" we yelled. "The play hasn't started yet!"

Jimmy apparently did not hear us as he continued to wrestle for the ball. We eventually unpiled Jimmy and the other team's center. The teams huddled again. I decided to try and give Jimmy an easier assignment.

"Jimmy," I said, "on this play you cover Andrew." Andrew was a younger boy, only about ten. "Wherever Andrew goes, you go with him. Don't let him catch the ball. Do you understand, Jimmy? Don't let him catch the ball."

Jimmy shook his head up and down enthusiastically. "*Yeth!*" he said.

"And Jimmy, let the center hike the ball to the quarterback. The play doesn't start until the quarterback has the ball. Okay?"

Jimmy kept nodding his head.

I lined Jimmy up opposite Andrew. I noticed that poor Andrew fidgeted a little when he saw Jimmy across from him. The center hiked the ball to the quarterback and he dropped back to pass. The quarterback turned and threw the ball toward Andrew.

Jimmy didn't necessarily understand the concept of pass interference. I don't think anyone even attempted to explain that rule to Jimmy. As the ball was in the air, I looked across the field and saw that Jimmy was covering Andrew pretty closely. In fact, he had Andrew locked in a full bear hug. Andrew's arms were pinned to his side. Jimmy was draped all over him. The ball was well thrown - right at Andrew. It hit Jimmy in the back and dropped harmlessly to the ground. Jimmy released Andrew and jumped on top of the ball.

Young Andrew, who hadn't played many games with Jimmy, yelled, "Hey! That's pass interference! He can't do that!"

We kind of shrugged but we had to agree with Andrew. We gave Andrew's team a pass interference penalty with a first down.

In the huddle, I thought about explaining the rule of pass interference to Jimmy. As I began to open my mouth, I looked at Jimmy's focused and enthusiastic face. A feeling of futility swept over me.

"Jimmy," I said. "You cover Andrew again, but don't hold him. Okay? Stay with him, but don't hold him."

Jimmy shook his head in acknowledgment.

On the next play, Andrew, now savvy of Jimmy's defensive technique, stepped backwards a couple of steps at the beginning of the play. Jimmy charged forward. Andrew then ran around Jimmy, and broke wide open. Andrew caught a pass, and ran for a touchdown.

Andrew stood in the end zone holding the ball, both hands raised in the air. Jimmy, who had been turned around during the play, took off running toward Andrew. Andrew's celebration abruptly ended when he saw Jimmy bearing down on him. Andrew started running again and sprinted across the field with Jimmy close behind him. He was screaming, "The play is over! The play is over!"

Jimmy, who didn't seem to hear Andrew, kept up his hot pursuit. Although Jimmy was not tall, he was strong and muscular. Jimmy could be pretty intimidating to a 9 or 10 year old boy. As Andrew was running for his life across the field, I was reminded of the second important lesson of playing football with Jimmy. That lesson was this: Jimmy was the most important person on the field. It was essential to know where Jimmy was at all times. If you were smaller than Jimmy, you only had to be flattened once or twice to learn this lesson. Otherwise, you were liable to be blind sided by him at a time when you least expected it. A young kid playing football with Jimmy experienced an interesting mix of amusement, curiosity and fear.

Andrew was running out of breath as Jimmy chased him. Andrew finally turned and heaved the ball back at Jimmy as if to say, "Here, you can have it!" Jimmy jumped on the ball and held it in the air as if it was a treasure that he had just recovered. He beamed with self-satisfaction.

We finally restored order and awarded Andrew's team the touchdown. It was now time for the other team to kick off.

"Jimmy," I said, "I will try to get the ball and hand it to you. I'll block for you. You take the ball and run for a touchdown. Do you understand?"

Jimmy shook his head vigorously. He had heard the word "touchdown" and he knew that touchdowns were very good. "*Yeah unnertan*" Jimmy said. He smiled.

The other team kicked the ball. I got to it, and handed it to Jimmy. Jimmy took off running, but saw Jeff coming right toward him. Now Jeff was a pretty big guy. Jimmy didn't necessarily have an understanding of field position. He did though, have a good understanding of size and bulk. As Jeff bore down on him, Jimmy stopped, did a U-turn, and started running the opposite direction towards his own goal line. Jeff and the rest of his team stopped chasing Jimmy as they watched him running toward their goal line.

Everyone on Jimmy's team started shouting "Wrong way!" Jimmy, however, saw a remarkably clear path and he intended to take advantage of it. He ran as hard as he could. As he crossed the goal line, he held the ball in the air and celebrated as if he had scored a touchdown. In Jimmy's world, a touchdown was a touchdown. It didn't matter which goal line you crossed.

Jimmy's arms shot into the air. "*Tutdown!*" he shouted as he jumped up and down. "*Tutdown Tauburn!*" (Auburn was Jimmy's favorite football team). Jimmy dashed to his closest teammate, Joshua. As he approached Joshua, he leaped up onto Joshua, both legs straddling him holding the ball in the air. Joshua collapsed to the ground with Jimmy on top of him. Jimmy's joy was undiminished. *"Tutdown!"* he yelled again as he got up. He threw the ball as high in the air as he could with both hands.

No one had the heart to dampen Jimmy's joy. "Good touchdown, Jimmy!" I said. "Great play! Now it's our ball back here." I pointed to the spot where Jimmy had reversed his direction.

"Yeth!" Jimmy said, both arms pumping with his fists clenched and breathing heavily from his efforts.

We huddled. "Jimmy," I said, "you stand beside me. Joshua, you hike the ball. Jimmy, I'm going to give the ball to you and you run for a touchdown. The goal line is that way. Okay?"

I pointed toward our goal. "Jimmy, run that way, okay?"

Jimmy shook his head. *"Tutdown!"* he repeated. He was focused.

We lined up. Joshua hiked the ball to me and I handed it to Jimmy. Jimmy took off running for our goal line. As the opposition was closing in behind him though, Jimmy turned and ran straight for the sideline. Jimmy didn't necessarily understand the concept of out of bounds. He ran out of bounds by 10 or 15 yards. The pursuit stopped. Jimmy, however, did not. He kept on running as hard as he could. He came back onto the field near his goal line and crossed it while everyone else stood and watched him.

Jimmy commenced another joyous celebration. *"Tutdown!"* he yelled.

My brother-in-law, Mike, got into the spirit of the celebration. He ran up to Jimmy and yelled "Way to go, Jim-mayyy!"

Jimmy jumped up onto Mike, who held him, and raised a hand into the air with his index finger extended. *"Numma one!"* Jimmy shouted. *"Tauburn numma one!"*

"Number one!" Mike echoed.

Jimmy jumped down. "High five!" Mike yelled. He held up his hand.

Jimmy jumped as high as he could to slap Mike's hand. Jimmy's maximum vertical leap was only a couple of inches, but it was enthusiastic. As he slapped Mike's hand, his pinky finger was extended out from the rest of his fingers, almost like some socialites do when they drink tea. Jimmy was not a very sophisticated person in many areas, but he had etiquette when it came to "high fives."

After the celebration subsided, we put the ball back where Jimmy had run out of bounds. In the huddle, Jimmy was still excited. "*Two tutdown!*" Jimmy exclaimed, still breathing heavily from his exertions.

"Okay," I said. "On this play, Jimmy you be the quarterback. Joshua will hike the ball to you, and you run the ball. We'll block for you." Jimmy nodded his head. "And Jimmy," I continued, "run toward the swing set. Our goal line is toward the swing set. Do you understand? Don't run that way [I pointed toward the sideline] or that way [I pointed back toward the other goal line]."

"*Wingthet.*" Jimmy repeated.

"Right, Jimmy. Run toward the swing set."

We broke the huddle and I placed Jimmy back behind Joshua. Joshua hiked the ball to Jimmy and he took off toward the swing set. Our blocking briefly worked and Jimmy had a little running room. The other team, however, began to close in on Jimmy. Just as Jon was about to tag him, Jimmy held the ball with both hands in front of him and heaved the ball toward the swing set as if throwing the ball across the goal line was just as good as running it there. Both teams scrambled for the ball, with Jimmy right in the midst of the melee.

For the rest of the afternoon, the game continued in a similar vein. Every play was different, and the only constant was Jimmy's unpredictable reaction each time. Team sports with Jimmy were freewheeling events. We had a nickname for it, derived from the star of the game. We called it "Jimball." At the end of a game of Jimball, we rarely knew who won. We rarely knew what the score was. We just knew that Jimball was different than any other game we had ever seen or played.

We visited Jimmy many times in my childhood. Jimmy and I played scores of football games together when we were young. We continued to play football as well as other sports as we grew older.

When I visited, Jimmy would say "*Davy, pway fooball at ole houth?*"

I replied, "Yes Jimmy, we played football at the old house."

Jimmy asked, "'*Core tutdown?*"

"Yes, Jimmy, we scored a lot of touchdowns."

"*Davy, ole buddy?*"

"Yes Jim, old buddy. We had some good times together, didn't we, buddy?"

"*Davy, weaaaaaaal ole buddy?*"

"Yes Jimmy, real old buddy."

Jimmy would just smile as he patted my back.

CHAPTER THREE
HUBBA HUBBA

Uncle Thomas says:
When Jimmy was young and he would play something, he only had one speed. That speed was all out. Jimmy did not understand the meaning of the words "slow" or "take it easy."

When Jimmy was eleven or twelve, Papa and Meme bought him a bicycle. Of course, the experts had said that Jimmy would never ride a bicycle or be able to do anything that required good balance or coordination. As he often did, Jimmy proved them wrong. He would get on that bike and pedal furiously. His legs would go pumping up and down on those pedals like pistons. He had his share of crashes. But that would not keep him from getting right back on that bike and going at it again.

Jimmy also drove a go-kart, but he only did that one time. Tim bought a go-kart and we brought it home. The older boys fixed it up and were driving it around. After awhile, someone had the idea that we should let Jimmy try it out. We put Jimmy in the go-kart and showed him what we could. I don't think he ever had a clue of what the brake was for, but he understood that the accelerator would make it go. When we started that go-kart, Jimmy pushed the accelerator to the floor and took off, weaving around the yard. He kept that accelerator down as far as he could as we chased after him. There is no telling where he would have ended up if there had not been a big tree right in the middle of the yard. Jimmy rammed that go-kart into that tree head on. He was a little shook up, but he was okay. He sat in the go-kart and turned and looked at us with a baffled expression that said "Who in the world would put an oak tree right in the middle of a go-kart track? That is one of the dumbest things I have ever seen in my life."

That was Jimmy's last solo go-kart ride.

Jimmy didn't mind trying new things. His mental capability was very limited. But the same disability may have freed him from fearful limitations caused by consequences foreseen by "normal" children.

In this regard, Jimmy fit in well with the Martin family. The family did not have a lot of money, and the children did not have a lot of toys. However, the family did have humor and they had creativity. Grandaddy was a very creative person, and he passed on that creativity to his children. In his lifetime, Grandaddy came up with a number of new ideas and inventions.

For most of his life, Grandaddy worked in farming and in construction. In the mid-1940's though, Grandaddy worked in a factory making commodes. While he was there, he thought of an idea of how to vent fumes away from a commode.

Grandaddy used to say:

One time I came up with a way to keep commode fumes from stinking up the bathroom. I put a vent pipe from the commode to the attic. The pipe had an exhaust fan in it that would draw the fumes from the toilet itself through the pipe and blow them into the attic.

One day, a friend, Leroy Garrett, was visiting us. I said, "Leroy, let me show you something I've been working on." I took him up to the attic and told him to sit there while I demonstrated the device.

I went back down to the bathroom and turned on the exhaust fan. I then sat down and used the commode. After a little bit, I heard Leroy up in the attic go "Whoo-wee! It stinks up here! What in the world are you doing down there?"

That little device worked. When you turned it on, you couldn't smell anything in the bathroom. It sure did stink up the attic though!

Another time, Grandaddy got tired of the amount of time that it took to pass serving dishes at the Martin dinner table. By the time that all eleven family members had been served, the food was cold. Grandaddy came up with the idea of putting a revolving "lazy susan" in the middle of the dinner table. That way, instead of having to pass a serving dish around to the person who wanted it, each person could just turn the "lazy susan" and get the food he wanted.

Jimmy's willingness to try new things helped him adapt to the Martin household. One summer we visited Alabama. Alabama summers were extremely hot, and Grandaddy and Grandmother did not have air conditioning. We boys and Jimmy decided that we wanted to sleep on the floor down in the basement where it was cooler. The basement had spiders and we even killed an occasional scorpion. Somehow though, the "wildlife" down there only added to the charm of the adventure.

We took a couple of fans down with us. We attached sheets to the top of the fans. When we turned the fans on, the sheets billowed and made "tents" for us to sleep in. Jimmy loved the tents. For years after that, he wanted to sleep under the "fan tents" in the basement.

Another reason that Jimmy loved the "tents" was that Jimmy was an extremely social person. He loved human interaction. He loved to belong. Given the number of children in the Martin household, human interaction was a frequent occurrence, and that suited Jimmy just fine.

Jimmy loved to play games and he loved playmates. One childhood game Jimmy loved was the "Hubba Hubba" game. Often, his face brightened and he said *"Yeah know. Hubba Hubba dame!"*

He would then turn to me and say *"Davy, you 'memba Hubba Hubba dame?"*

Actually, I didn't remember the Hubba Hubba game. The Hubba Hubba game occurred before my time. But I had heard about it a hundred times from Jimmy. I would say "Yes, Jimmy, I know about the Hubba Hubba game."

Jimmy shared a bedroom with the younger boys of the family - Uncle Daniel, Uncle Andy, and Uncle Thomas. Uncle Thomas was the youngest child of the family - three years younger than Jimmy. But Jimmy and Uncle Thomas were close playmates.

One day, Jimmy and Uncle Thomas discovered the trampoline effect of the mattresses in their bedroom. They bounced up and down on the mattresses, tumbling from bed to bed. As they jumped, they yelled, "Hubba Hubba!" The phrase "Hubba Hubba!" did not have any particular meaning. It simply expressed their exhilaration as they bounced around like gymnasts on their bedroom furniture. Thus, this gymnastic exercise became the Hubba Hubba game.

The Hubba Hubba game went on for quite a while. Unfortunately, the Hubba Hubba game had a negative consequence. Jimmy and Uncle Thomas jumped so long and with such vigor that they bent the metal mattress rails on their beds. They didn't just bend the rails a little bit. The centers of the rails were almost touching the floor and their mattresses took on a concave shape.

Jimmy also often said "No like trouble." Bending the mattress rails on their beds caused some "trouble." Whatever consequences Jimmy and Uncle Thomas incurred as a result of the Hubba Hubba game though, did not diminish the pleasure of its memory for Jimmy.

Nicknames abounded in the Martin household. They were part of the humor and creativity used by the family to relate to each other and to entertain.

The nickname for Rachel (my mother) was "Turtle." When Uncle Daniel was little, he couldn't pronounce "Rachel," and it sounded for all the world like "Turtle." The name stuck. Sometimes when Jimmy saw his sister, Rachel, he said *"Lurtal, lurtal, lur-talll!"* Jimmy let the nickname roll slowly over his tongue in an affectionate, lilting tone.

Uncle Mark's nickname was "Jones," which was short for Rastus B. Jones. Mark was occasionally called "Rastus."

Uncle Stephen's nickname as a child was "Two-bits" – the old phrase for twenty-five cents. (Uncle Stephen would become a Certified Public Accountant).

Uncle David had a nickname of "Ky-er."

Uncle Tim's nickname was "Cash" (he held two jobs most of his life).

Grandaddy's pet name for Aunt Rebecca was "Bucky." This nickname was an affectionate variation of her name, Rebecca. When Aunt Rebecca was a little girl, if she was asked her name, she proclaimed "I Bucky!" We nephews called Aunt Rebecca – "Aunt Roe."

Uncle Daniel first became an uncle at age 8. He was so gleeful at the prospect of becoming an uncle that his brothers started calling him "Unc," and the nickname stuck.

Uncle Andy was tall (6'5"), thin and lanky. His nickname was "Sick." After we went hiking with our long-legged Uncle Andy one time though, we nephews started calling him the "Jolly Green Giant." Uncle Andy's nephews loved to play with him.

Uncle Thomas was also skinny as a child. His nickname was "Skin."

The person responsible for assigning most of the nicknames was the oldest boy, Uncle Mark. None of the Martin nicknames, though, surpassed the nickname of the girl that Uncle Mark married. Her name was Gail, but somewhere along the line she acquired the nickname of "Pickles."

Jimmy did not care for any of his early nicknames. His given name was James Carlton Stuckey, Jr. James Carlton was shortened to "J.C." Jimmy did not like this nickname. If you said to Jimmy "Hey! J.C.!," his face twisted in disgust and he said *"No know him."*

Jimmy's disdain of the name "J.C." did not approach his extreme distaste for its expanded form – "Jiminy Cricket." If you said to Jimmy "Hey Jiminy Cricket!" he shook his head vigorously and said *"Pweeeath! No my weal* (real) *name. No lite* (like) *Jim'ny Kwicket! Weal HATE Jim'ny Kwicket!"*

Eventually, Jimmy did acquire a nickname that he liked, and it was used frequently and affectionately. That nickname was "George." The origin of the nickname "George" is somewhat uncertain, although most family members believe that the nickname originated with me.

When I was young, I loved the children's book character, Curious George. Curious George was a monkey whose curiosity got him into trouble in every story. Invariably, Curious George found some way to redeem himself at the end of each book.

My sister, Sharon, tells me that I had a pet stuffed monkey named Curious George when I was young. I remember a stuffed monkey. That monkey was named after Jimmy, but its name was "Jim-Jim." I had Jim-Jim in my room until I went off to college. In any event, the love of Curious George resulted in the nickname of "George" for Jimmy and it stuck.

When the nickname "George" was used, it was often done affectionately in a kind of lilting tone. Years later, Jimmy's boyhood roommate, Uncle Thomas, often greeted Jimmy "Hey Geooorrrguh!"

Jimmy responded accordingly in a slow, tender voice, *"Hey Tommm-bus!"*

Jimmy then added *"Tommm-bus! Tombus my brudda ole houth!"* ("Thomas my brother at the old house").

"You're my brother Geooorrrguh!"
"Lub you, Tommm-bus!"
"I love you, Geoorrguh!"
"Tommm-bus!"

The years did not erode the bonds of companionship forged during childhood.

CHAPTER FOUR
ONE TRACK

Living with Jimmy was a challenge. Jimmy had to make significant adjustments when he came to live with the Martin family. The family had to make huge adjustments as well.

Jimmy made some unusual noises. Jimmy compressed air in the back of his throat and then released it. It sounded all the world like a pig grunting. We called it the "pig noise." Jimmy would not just do it once or twice. He could "do the pig" for hours.

Jimmy also ground his teeth. When he wasn't grinding his teeth, he chomped his teeth together continuously. It sounded like the clip-clop of a horse coming down the street. We called it his "horse noise." For his whole life, Jimmy's teeth were short, about half the length of normal teeth, due to the grinding and chomping.

Jimmy was a creature of habit. He did the "pig" and the "horse" noises subconsciously, almost by reflex. If Jimmy wasn't talking, it was usually the pig or the horse. We used to make jokes about life with Jimmy being "down on the farm."

The "pig" and the "horse" were kind of funny sounds for the first 30 seconds. After a while, though, they got on a person's nerves. The sounds just went on and on - streaming through the atmosphere all around Jimmy. Different family members tried to get Jimmy to stop doing the noises, but he really didn't realize he was doing it.

Jimmy would be grunting like a pig. Meme would say "Jimmy, do I hear a pig?"

Jimmy stopped grunting and said *"Oh! Thorry!"*

There was silence for a few minutes. Then, we heard a horse clopping down the street. The poor guy really couldn't help himself.

Jimmy loved music. When he was young, the Martin family attended the church led by Jimmy Glenn, whom Jimmy called "Big Jimmy." One of "little Jimmy's" favorite songs was *"Deep and Wide."*

Deep and wide,
Deep and wide,
There's a fountain flowing
Deep and wide...

"Deep and Wide" had repetition and Jimmy liked that aspect. But the song also had hand motions to make with it. "Big Jimmy" taught "little Jimmy" to stand in front of the congregation and to lead the singing of *"Deep and Wide."* Jimmy liked the idea of moving to music.

Music charmed Jimmy. He moved and rocked his body to the rhythm. When he was young, someone gave him a transistor radio. Jimmy loved his transistor radio. He put it to his ear and listened to the music while sitting on the floor. Jimmy rocked back and forth, dipping his head low between his legs. He rocked to the beat for hours, moving to the music. The endless rocking helped make Jimmy a very limber person. He could sit on the ground, stretch out his legs, and touch his nose to the floor between his legs.

Jimmy liked the songs of his teenage years - the "old songs" he later called them. Songs about characters like *Big, Bad John* and songs about cars like the *Hot...Rod...Lincoln*. In later years when younger and "hipper" family members enthused about the great "new" songs by groups like the Beatles, Jimmy argued with them about the "best" music. He would say, *"Lite ole songs best."*

Jimmy also loved to swing. He took his radio out to the swing set with him. Jimmy put the radio to his ear with his arm around the swing chain, and started swinging ... back and forth, back and forth, back and forth. Jimmy swung for hours listening to his music. After he had been swinging awhile, he held the radio out in front of him in his palm, pinning the swing chain to his side with his elbow. The rhythm of the music and the movement of the swing had a soothing effect. It gave Jimmy a feeling of freedom.

The repetition of movement built some very strong muscles. Jimmy was short, but he was extremely strong. Anyone who wrestled with Jimmy quickly realized that he was no weakling. Because of this strength, Jimmy was the designated ice cream maker when we were young. (Jimmy called it "*ifream*.") The Martin family had an old fashioned, hand cranked ice cream maker. The young children gathered on the back porch, trying to turn the crank. As the ice cream froze, the crank became harder to turn. We children could only turn the handle a few times. Jimmy could crank from start to finish without stopping - hundreds of turns of the handle - over and over again. Jimmy enjoyed his status as the designated ice cream maker. He received a lot of encouragement and thanks. Not many things taste better than cold homemade ice cream on a hot summer day in the deep South.

Repetition was Jimmy's friend. Perhaps the area in which he was the most repetitive was his conversation. Jimmy's mind was not the most agile. Jimmy didn't have a broad range of conversation topics. What topics he did have though, were firmly imprinted.

Jimmy could talk through his normal range of conversation topics in about five minutes. Conversation was a means of relationship for Jimmy, and Jimmy loved relationship. After talking for the first five minutes, Jimmy went back and started the same topics over again. To Jimmy, something was just as interesting the hundredth time as it was the first time. Jimmy didn't understand why his listener did not want to hear the same thing over and over and over again.

If the listener became a little agitated upon hearing the same story the third or fourth time around, Jimmy only tried harder to convey the information. Often, the beleaguered listener tried to change the topic. Jimmy would have none of that. A person couldn't distract him off of his subjects. We joked that Jimmy's train only ran on one track. The train ran early and it ran often, and it never jumped track.

If we were at the dinner table and Jimmy was streaming through his topics, Grandaddy would finally tell Jimmy not to mention a subject again. This instruction frustrated Jimmy, but he obeyed Papa.

When we visited Alabama, warm greetings and good feelings always abounded on the first day. We tried to listen to Jimmy's "broken record" conversation intently and lovingly. The next day, the charm of Jimmy's conversation diminished somewhat. By the third or fourth day, it could get real old. Old or not, Jimmy relentlessly focused on his topics.

The person who bore the brunt of Jimmy's repetition was Grandmother. Grandaddy worked extremely hard all day trying to feed his large family. For most of his life, he worked construction with some farming on the side. He got up and left for work before dawn, and often did not return home until after dark.

Grandmother stayed at home. She cooked, cleaned, washed, ironed and took care of the young children. She also took care of Jimmy. She was around him for hours on end, listening to his sounds and hearing his conversation - day after day after day. More than once one of my uncles has said, "I don't know how Meme ever did it." That uncle would pause, and then say, "She was a person who had faith."

Grandmother was a person of great patience and she showed great compassion. I only saw Grandmother ill with Jimmy one time. Jimmy had been having problems with his eyesight. In order to have

Jimmy's eyes tested, the family set up an appointment with a pediatric optometrist. The visit to the optometrist alone could be a challenge. Uncle Tim recalls one visit to the optometrist.

Uncle Tim says:

A trip to the optometrist with Jimmy was something else. Jimmy's eyesight was getting worse. We called to set up an appointment with a pediatric optometrist. We explained Jimmy's situation to the optometrist. The optometrist said that his office handled special needs patients all the time and that the eye exam would take approximately thirty minutes. He said an examination of Jimmy should not pose any problem. He obviously didn't know who he was dealing with. After a little time with Jimmy, I think he realized that he was just a little overconfident about the exam.

When we took Jimmy to his appointment, the assistant took us into an examining room. The optometrist came in and began the exam. Instead of letters on the eye chart, they had animals. Young children can't identify letters, but they can recognize animals, and Jimmy did know his animals. The optometrist would point to an animal and ask Jimmy if he could tell him what it was. But Jimmy wasn't interested in identifying the animal. If it was a cat, Jimmy started talking about "Kit-cat" or some other animal that Jimmy had known. If the optometrist tried to stop Jimmy or to proceed with the exam - well, you know how Jimmy is when some one doesn't listen or tries to change the subject. He just keeps telling the same story and repeating what he wants to say over and over. You can't change the conversation on Jimmy.

And so that's the way it was during the whole exam - back and forth. The optometrist trying to conduct the exam, and Jimmy telling the optometrist what Jimmy wanted the optometrist to hear. The poor optometrist was fighting a losing battle. Jimmy was interacting the same way he would with any other person.

After a session with Jimmy that lasted about an hour and a half, a rather flustered optometrist gave up and said, "I am not sure what we accomplished in there. I think that we have an eyeglass prescription that is about as close as we can get. I don't have any idea if it is the right prescription, but I have really done about all I can do."

After the prolonged visit to the pediatric optometrist, the family went to an optical store and had Jimmy fitted for glasses. Selecting anything with Jimmy was not easy. Jimmy tried on frame after frame in order to find one that suited him. Meme finally found a pair of glasses that Jimmy would tolerate and that the family could afford, and they all went home. Meme carefully instructed Jimmy on the use and care of his glasses.

On the same afternoon that Jimmy came home with his new glasses, he managed to sit or step on them. They were broken irreparably. Grandmother had had it. She said, "Jimmy, I just can't believe after all that work and all we told you about caring for your glasses, that you would break them in the same day that you got them. That just makes me sick."

Those words "[T]hat just makes me sick" were remarkable. They were not remarkable for the moment. At that moment, they were appropriate. They expressed the frustration and exasperation of the situation. They expressed exactly how Grandmother felt. The reason that those words were remarkable is those were the harshest words that I ever heard my Grandmother speak in her whole life - to Jimmy or to anyone else.

CHAPTER FIVE
MY HOUSE FIRST

Uncle Daniel says:
Jimmy was a little wild when he first came to live with us. He was also really fast. He knew how sweet brown sugar was and he loved to eat it. Jimmy would sneak into the kitchen, and before you knew it, he grabbed a bag of brown sugar. He took off and ran underneath the house with it. He crawled way back under the house with it so that an adult could not reach him. Jimmy sat under there and ate the brown sugar. Daddy (Grandaddy) sent one of us younger boys under there to get him. There were spiders and worms and lizards under there. Going underneath the house to retrieve Jimmy wasn't any fun.

When we finally pulled him out, then Daddy would get his belt. Boy, he would use it too.

But Jimmy responded to the belt. God knew what he was doing when he put Jimmy in a family with Papa and Meme. Papa gave him the firm discipline that he needed, and Meme gave him the mercy and compassion that he needed.

Jimmy's boyhood habit of crawling under the house or exploring obscure places got him in trouble at least one other time. While playing in a dank crawl space one day, he was bitten by a copperhead snake. Jimmy, however, did not understand the danger. For this reason, he did not get very upset, which may have saved his life. Agitation and the resulting increase in blood circulation can cause venom to spread through a person's body quickly. Jimmy only knew that the snake bite stung.

Jimmy was hospitalized for a few days due to his snake bite. He had to undergo a long series of antivenom shots to treat it. Two kind hospital nurses, Bea and Gypsy, brought him milkshakes to help soothe the trauma. For the rest of his life, Jimmy had a very healthy fear of snakes.

Thereafter, Jimmy often teased someone else about snakes. He curled his first two fingers like fangs and said *"Nate bite!* (Snake bite!) *Toppahead nate."* He then struck with his arm as if it were a snake biting someone. This simulated strike was followed by the inevitable "Shot in seat" which let everyone know to which part of Jimmy's anatomy his antivenom shots had been administered.

Whenever Jimmy walked in the woods or any place where there was underbrush, he walked very circumspectly. He took high steps and trod very gingerly, carefully inspecting the area where he was walking. He hated to retrieve balls that rolled down into the woods. Jimmy would be the last person to volunteer to go get a ball in the woods, even if he was the person that threw or kicked the ball down there. *"You doe head"* (You go ahead) he would say, as if he were politely allowing you to be the one to go retrieve the ball from the snaky woods.

Just as the Martin family had to adjust to Jimmy, Jimmy had to make huge adjustments when he came to live with the Martin family. Not only was he living with a strange family, but the method of order and discipline was much stricter than Jimmy had previously experienced. But Jimmy responded to the discipline - probably in large part because it was encased in love and supported by relationship.

Grandaddy was a strong disciplinarian. I never saw Jimmy get spanked. The threat of Grandaddy's belt, however, had enough impact that I assumed there had been some meaningful "woodshed" moments in Jimmy's younger days. Most times when Jimmy was acting up, Grandaddy could just point to his belt buckle and look at

Jimmy. The change in Jimmy's demeanor was immediate and palpable.

Although I never saw him spanked, I did see Jimmy get "time out" when an attitude adjustment was in order. Once or twice I even saw him "miss a meal." Jimmy loved to eat. If he strayed too far, Grandaddy would tell him that he was going to miss the next meal. This discipline was crushing to Jimmy, and given the quality of Meme's cooking, I can't say that I blame him.

When he had to miss a meal, Jimmy acted as if he was under a heavy sentence. Jimmy had character though, and he would rally. As we stood facing the mirror together on one such occasion, he said, *"Be otay, Davy. Yeah be all right."* He was either reassuring himself, or insuring that I didn't worry about him too much - and it may have been a little of both. I did notice that Grandaddy and Grandmother did not eat during the next meal as well.

Grandaddy could be strict and authoritarian. At times, he seemed overbearing. Grandaddy was a tall man and he was an imposing figure. He had survived the Great Depression, and he had seen some hard times in his life. Those hard times forced him to eke out what was called a "hard scrabble" living. But he learned about love in his life, and he grew in it. Grandaddy once told me that his wife was the person that taught him to love.

Grandmother did not administer spankings. She had a different means of influence. Grandmother served every person around her. She genuinely cared about the needs of others, and tried to meet them as best she could. Her character was sterling, and it encouraged imitation. Grandmother's example prompted persons around her to serve others as well.

Grandmother brought out the best in people. She saw the positive traits in others and she encouraged and emphasized those traits. Grandmother rarely said anything negative about anyone. She looked for the best attributes in every person she met. Her perspective motivated others to do their best, and to nurture their gifts and positive qualities.

Grandaddy and Grandmother had different styles and different strengths. It wasn't that one approach was right and the other wrong. Sometimes judgement is needed, and sometimes mercy is needed. Grandaddy and Grandmother learned to work together as a team in life, and they learned from each other. Their combined parentage was exactly what Jimmy needed in his life, and it helped produce indelible character.

When Jimmy came to the Martin family in 1955, they lived in a rented farm house in Montgomery, Alabama. It was located off of Narrow Lane Road. Jimmy called the house the *"Nawoh Lane Woad houth,"* or simply the *"Weal ol' houth."*

The Narrow Lane Road house was located on a chicken and cattle farm. It was initially built as a summer house. It had a large central living room, with three bedrooms and one bathroom off the living room. The location of the bathroom indicated that indoor plumbing had been installed after the house had been built. The bathroom stood in a hallway and it had three doors. In fact, the back bedroom could be accessed from the inside only *through* the bathroom.

A single, three door bathroom serving the needs of eleven people presented some challenges. On one occasion, a visitor to the house referred to any bathroom occupant as a "victim." The Martin family, however, did not mind the arrangement too terribly. They had lived a number of other places that had no bathrooms, just outhouses. A house with an indoor bathroom was considered somewhat of a luxury. The family lived at the Narrow Lane Road house for almost 13 years.

Jimmy first lived with the Martin family on a trial basis. He was taken in by them out of necessity, not convenience. The Martin's initially agreed to keep Jimmy for two weeks. But Jimmy gradually fit into the family. Two weeks led to two more weeks, which led to a month, which led to a year. Jimmy was never legally adopted. After a couple of years though, he became a part of the family, and no one in the Martin family questioned whether he should live anywhere else.

One day I was at the kitchen table talking with Grandmother and Jimmy about old family friends. I heard the name and stories of one friend after another. After awhile, Jimmy's face lit up and he said *"Yeah know - Eo Witwuh!"* He then smiled as if sharing a pleasant thought.

I said, "What?" Jimmy looked at me as if something was wrong with me.

He repeated, "*Eo Witwuh!*"

Grandmother smiled at my puzzlement and said, "Jimmy is saying 'Leo Whitworth.'"

I asked, "Who is Leo Whitworth?"

Grandmother said:

Leo Whitworth was a school friend of Mark's who visited us often. He did something one day that Jimmy has always remembered.

After Jimmy had been with us a few years, we had another young man who came to live with us for a while. His name was Joe Lopez. Joe was a troubled child but, like Jimmy when he came to us, Joe really didn't have any other place to go.

Joe did not fit in to our family the way that Jimmy did. Joe and Jimmy didn't get along. In fact, Joe didn't really get along well with anyone. He could be very aggravating, and he got into fights a lot. He would aggravate someone and when that person would respond

to the aggravation, it usually resulted in an argument or a fight. Although he was happy to be here, I don't think that Jimmy liked the idea of another person coming in, especially some one as difficult as Joe.

Anyway, some of our boys and Joe and Jimmy were playing near the pond at the Narrow Lane Road house in Montgomery. Leo Whitworth was also there with them. Joe was acting up, and he started aggravating Leo Whitworth. Leo took it for a while, but then he finally had enough. Leo went over, picked Joe up, and threw him right into the pond.

This action pleased Jimmy to no end. When Leo dumped Joe into the pond, Jimmy jumped up and down gleefully. Then he yelled at Joe "Now you learn! MY HOUSE FIRST!"

And so it was.

CHAPTER SIX
DILIGENCE IN LEARNING

Jimmy had the mental capability of a five year old child. Although he had higher function in some other areas, his ability to understand and to reason was severely limited.

A number of persons, including myself, tried to help Jimmy learn and develop mentally. One of his primary teachers was Jimmy's niece (my sister), Sharon. Sharon had a couple of distinct advantages over the rest of us. Sharon actually had training and certification in the field of special education.

More importantly, Sharon was a talented and pretty blonde. She knew when to kiss, when to hug, when to cajole and when to scold. Jimmy liked to be cajoled and encouraged by pretty blondes. He especially liked to be kissed and hugged by pretty blondes. For these reasons, and many more, Sharon occupied a special place in Jimmy's heart during his whole life. If Sharon wanted to try to teach Jimmy something, Jimmy was at least willing to make an effort.

On one teaching occasion, Sharon wanted to enhance Jimmy's verbal comprehension. She said, "Now, Jimmy, listen to me, Sugar. We are going to play a word game. Okay?"

Jimmy didn't look to me like he really wanted go through this exercise. Sharon, however, had called him "Sugar" and that alone assured his cooperation. He nodded his head in assent.

"Now, Jimmy, we are going to work with words that rhyme - words that sound alike. I will tell you two words. You need to think of two other words that say the same thing, but rhyme with each other."

The blank expression on Jimmy's face told me that he had no clue what Sharon had just said. He, however, was a captivated participant in this exercise and continued to give positive signals.

"Let me give you an example, Jimmy. If I said 'Large kitten,' what would you say?"

Jimmy still had a blank expression on his face.

"A large kitten, Jimmy. A large kitten is a faaat...." Sharon made a charades motion for Jimmy to finish the phrase.

Jimmy's clueless expression did not change.

"A large kitten is a faaat c...c..." Sharon sounded out a hard "c." "A fat c..." Sharon looked at Jimmy expectantly.

Blank expression.

"A large kitten, Jimmy. A laaarge kitten is a fat c... Go ahead and try honey."

Jimmy screwed his face with determination and closed his eyes. He sat and thought for a while. Imitation was all he had, and the word did start with a hard "c."

"*Titten*" he said.

"No, Sugar, that's a good try. But we want a word that sounds like fat. It sounds like fat and begins with a 'c.' Fat c...c...c...." Once again Sharon gave a series of hard "c's."

Jimmy made an effort. "*Fat...*" he said repeating Sharon. But no ideas came. "*Too hard*" Jimmy protested.

"Listen to me, Jimmy. A large kitten is a FAT CAT!"

"*TAT!*" Jimmy exclaimed as if the answer now made all the sense in the world.

"Do you understand now, Jimmy? Fat cat."

"*Yeah unnertan.*" Jimmy said dutifully. "*Fat TAT.*"

"Now, Jimmy," Sharon said. "Let's try one more, Honey, okay?"

Jimmy didn't look to me like he really wanted to try one more. But he now had "fat cat" and Sharon had called him "Honey," so he nodded his head "Yes."

"Now Jimmy, listen to the next clue." Jimmy closed his eyes. He was either concentrating, or praying. "The next clue is a 'warm place.' What is a warm place?"

Jimmy paused. He decided to go with prior success. "*Fat tat?*" he guessed.

"No, Jimmy, a warm place is not a fat cat. This is a different clue. I want you to try real hard. What is a warm place?"

Jimmy scrunched his face in determination again. He then gave me a look that begged for help. I wasn't about to interfere with my sister's efforts. Jimmy looked to the ceiling (and maybe beyond) for help and inspiration. None came.

"Listen to me, Jimmy. A warm place is a hot...." Sharon once again made the charades sign.

Jimmy copied the charades sign. "*Hot...*" he said as his eyes rolled around the room. No ideas came.

"Listen to me, Honey. A warm place is a hot ssssss......." Sharon extended her "s" with a hiss. "A hot ssss...."

Jimmy dutifully repeated the phrase. "*Hot sss....*" Jimmy's "sss" sounded more like "th," but he did the best "sss" that he could.

"Jimmy, the next word begins with an 's' - an 'SSSSSSSS' sound. A warm place is a hot sssss..."

Jimmy repeated the sound. He screwed up his face even harder and closed his eyes again. "*Hot sss....*"

"Come on, Jimmy!" Sharon said. "You can do it!"

Jimmy kept repeating the phrase for a couple of minutes. Then there was a long period of silence. Sharon continued to encourage him. "Think, Jimmy. Hot ssss...."

Suddenly, Jimmy opened his eyes and slowly unscrewed his face. His eyes got bigger, and for the first time all afternoon, they shined with the light of recognition. "*Yeah know*" he said as he started shaking his head up and down - slowly at first and then increasing in intensity. "*YEAH KNOW!*"

"Jimmy, that's great!" Sharon said. She started to get excited at the prospect of a break through. Jimmy began to smile. Enthusiastically, Sharon smiled too. "I knew you could do it. Jimmy, you tell me what a warm place is. A warm place is a hot sss...."

Jimmy smiled knowingly and, with the air of a man who was confident of the winning answer, said "*Hot SUMMER!*"

I looked at Sharon and she looked at me. I snorted. I couldn't contain my laughter. Only my respect for her and her disappointment prevented me from rolling in the floor. Jimmy was looking around the room triumphantly. Sharon put her head into her hands. She appeared completely deflated. Mustering all her composure, she said "That's good, Jimmy. But that is not the word we were looking for, Sugar. A warm place is a hot SPOT."

"*Hot 'POT!*" Jimmy repeated just as triumphantly as before. "*Hot summer! Hot 'pot!*" He was grinning from ear to ear.

"Jimmy, I think that is enough for now" Sharon said with a sigh. "You did -um- did very well, Sweetie."

Jimmy just beamed. Another successful lesson!

Over time I thought about Jimmy's answer. And you know, it made pretty good sense coming from a person who had endured numerous sweltering Alabama summers without the benefit of air conditioning.

Grandmother used to say:

When Jimmy first came to us, you could barely understand anything that he said. The experts told us that he would never be able to speak normally, and that he would never be able to communicate in a way that you could understand him. Well, you can see how wrong they were. We don't always understand exactly

what Jimmy says, but he is able to communicate. He will find a way to let you know what he is saying. Under the circumstances, Jimmy speaks wonderfully well.

Grandmother usually said this when we had difficulty understanding Jimmy, which was often. When something that Jimmy said stumped us, we would ask Grandmother. Grandmother usually, but not always, could tell us what Jimmy was saying. Once Jimmy told me *"Weal lite kiki."*

I said, "Real like what?"

Jimmy repeated, *"Weal lite kiki. Duuud kiki."*

"I don't understand Jimmy. What is kiki?"

At such times, Jimmy got frustrated. He began to shake his head and, in a self effacing manner, said *"Tan't talt pwain."* After a little more effort and frustration, however, Jimmy's "I can't talk plain" would change to "You can't hear plain." Jimmy didn't feel that he alone bore the responsibility for the inability to communicate.

Eventually, Jimmy gave up. *"Ast Meme"* he said, and I would go ask Grandmother. "Kiki" as it turns out, was Jimmy's favorite food at that time - chicken. If you ever saw him eat fried chicken, you would understand what he meant when he said *"Weal lite kiki."*

We spent a lot of time trying to help Jimmy with his speech. He worked at it and the work produced moderately successful results. After some determined effort, "kiki" became "shi....KEN." Jimmy pronounced it so that it was intelligible to most of us. But like a waiter in a Chinese restaurant who pauses before every word that he struggles to pronounce correctly, Jimmy stopped before trying to pronounce the word. I would ask, "Okay Jimmy, do you like chicken?"

Jimmy would say, *"Weal lite* (pregnant pause) *shi....KEN."* Then he would smile and nod his head at his achievement.

My most successful Jimmy speech project centered around a college football team. Jimmy loved football. More specifically, he loved the Auburn Tigers ("*Tauburn*"). Jimmy loved to talk about football. He could review the most recent football games for hours. Words like "Mississippi" or "Louisiana" were beyond Jimmy's ability to pronounce. For this reason, Jimmy had his own unique name for each football team. The Mississippi Rebels were "*Ol' Miff Rerelth.*"

"*Bulldoh Tate*" referred to the Mississippi State Bulldogs.

The Louisiana State Tigers were "*L Eth U Titers.*"

The Tennessee Volunteers were the "*Tensee Vol.*"

The Alabama Crimson Tide, Auburn's arch rival, was simply "*Woll Tide.*"

One day, Jimmy wanted to discuss football. He said, "*Davy, Vanbill looth.*"

I said, "What?"

Jimmy said, "*Vanbill looth.*"

I asked "Who lost Jimmy?"

Jimmy said, "*Vanbill looth. Tensee Vol. Tensee Vol beat Vanbill.*"

"Oh!" I said. "You mean Vanderbilt!"

Jimmy shook his head. "*Yeth! Vanbill looth.*"

For some teams, Jimmy used their nickname to help identify them. He never just said "Georgia." It was always "*Jorja Bulldoh.*" Vanderbilt's nickname, however, was the "Commodores." Jimmy could barely say "Vanderbilt." He wasn't about to tackle "Commodores."

"Jimmy," I said. "It's pronounced 'Vanderbilt.' Can you say 'Vanderbilt?'"

"*Vanbill.*"

"No, Jimmy. Listen closely. Van…der…bilt. Vanderbilt."

Jimmy said, "*Vanbill.*"

"No, Jimmy. Say 'Van...'"

"*Van...*"

"...derbilt."

"*Bill.*"

"Jimmy, lets try again. Van..."

"*Van...*"

"der..."

"*ler...*"

"Not 'ler.' Der...."

"*der...*"

"That's it Jimmy. Let's try again. Van..."

"*Van...*"

"der..."

"*der...*"

"bilt..."

"*bill...*"

"Okay Jimmy. Let's try to put it together. Van..der..bilt."

"*Van......ler........bill.*"

"Not Vanlerbill. Vanderbilt."

"*Van...ler...bill.*"

I never got Jimmy to say the "D" in Vanderbilt. It was always "*Van...ler...bill.*"

"Vanlerbill" was close enough though, and I was satisfied that "Vanlerbill" was a lot closer to Vanderbilt than "Vanbill."

Jimmy must have experienced some satisfaction as well. The next time I came down to Alabama to visit, Jimmy and I were talking not long after I had arrived. Jimmy held up his hand as if to stop me and said, "Wait!" He paused and then took a deep breath to focus as hard as he could. "*Van...ler...bill.*" He then smiled a smile of satisfied achievement.

I said, "That is really good, Jimmy. You are doing great."

Jimmy did have a hard time learning. He had significant learning disabilities. His mental disability, however, was not the only obstacle to his "education." If Jimmy did not want to learn something, it was nigh impossible to teach it to him.

Jimmy had two advantages if he did not want to learn something. First, he could deflect a question with ease. Second, he could repeat the answer he wanted to give ten, twenty, a hundred or even a thousand times if need be. Repetition was his strong suit, and it didn't bother him to use it. We used to joke that his real calling in life was as a presidential press secretary.

I made many well-intentioned, but probably misguided, attempts to assist Jimmy. One time I decided that current events and news might be helpful to Jimmy. Looking back, I can't recall what prompted this decision. Nonetheless, I acted on it - only to be stymied by the man that we labeled the "master."

"Now, Jimmy" I began. "Do you know the name of the President of the United States?"

"*What?*"

"Think, Jimmy. The President of the United States. Do you know his name?"

"*No know him.*"

"Jimmy, I know you don't know him. I want to know if you know his name."

"*Too hard.*"

"Now, Jimmy think. Who is in charge of our country right now?"

Jimmy shook his head and heaved a sigh. "*You doe 'head.*"

"Okay, Jimmy, now listen. The President of the United States is a man named George Bush."

"*Whaaat?*"

"The President is named George Bush."

"*No know him.*"

"Jimmy, I know that you don't know him. I want you to learn his name. His name is George Bush."

"*You thure?*"

I heaved a sigh. "Yes, Jimmy, I am sure. Now, if I asked you who the President of the United States is, what would you say?"

"*Man in da moon.*" This last answer was accompanied by a shrug of the shoulders and a slight smile. Jimmy was toying with me now.

"Listen, Jimmy, I'm serious here. I want you to learn this. This man is very important. He is in charge of our country. The President of the United States is named George Bush. Can you say 'George Bush?'"

"*Too hard ta learn.*"

"Now, Jimmy, it is not too hard. What is the name of the President of the United States?"

"*No know him.*"

"Listen George…" and at this moment Jimmy's nickname gave me inspiration for a new approach. "Listen George, he has the same name as you do. His first name is George, just like your name."

"*Whaaat?*"

"It's true. He is a 'George.' too. The President of the United States! They call him George just like you! His name is George Bush."

"*You thure?*"

"Sure I'm sure. He has the same name as my old buddy, George," I said, trying some relational appeal. I couldn't call Jimmy "Honey" or "Sugar" like Sharon, but at least I had "Buddy." "So if I asked you 'What is the name of the President of the United States?' what would you say, Buddy?"

"*Too hard.*"

"Jimmy, it's not too hard. All you have to say is 'George Bush.' Nothing hard about that."

"You doe 'head."

"No, Jimmy, I want you to do it. What is the name of the President of the United States?"

"No know him."

And it would go on as long as I could last. Jimmy was willing to run around this track as many times as I was. He was just as fresh as the first time, while I was wearing out. My frustration levels rose while Jimmy blithely supplied blank repetition. If he ever muttered the words "George Bush," I don't recall it.

The only lesson learned that day was by me. I only thought that I was the teacher.

Later in his life, Jimmy expressed a desire to go to school. A number of his brothers had graduated from college, and Jimmy wanted to attend school as well. Grandmother was willing to try to teach him. She obtained some pre-school, kindergarten, and first grade materials. Every morning at about ten o'clock, she and Jimmy worked for an hour or two on his "lessons." They worked on letters, numbers, and writing. Grandmother then read to Jimmy. One of his favorite books was Hurlbut's Children's Bible story book.

Jimmy did not ever learn how to read. He couldn't. I don't think he even learned the whole alphabet. Jimmy did, however, learn how to write his name, and he learned how to write the phrase "I love you." He wrote each letter of the alphabet slowly and meticulously. Jimmy was very proud of this accomplishment, and wrote "I love you Jimmy" to a number of people. The phrase would be written 30 or 40 times on one page.

Jimmy also learned how to count. He could count as high as 11 or 12 before he began to lose track.

Jimmy's "school" went on for a number of months. Jimmy memorized some words and phrases, but he did not go beyond a kindergarten level of cognition.

Uncle Daniel was a pastor in Selma, and also served as principal at a private school, Bethel Christian School. After many months of learning, the family arranged for Jimmy to have a "Graduation Ceremony" at Bethel Christian School. Grandaddy and Grandmother drove Jimmy from Wetumpka to Bethel Christian School in Selma.

At the ceremony, Uncle Daniel made some remarks about Jimmy and about his schooling. Jimmy then "marched" and received his "diploma." Thus, on May 18, 1990, a forty year old Downs Syndrome man received a Certificate for "Diligence in Learning" in Selma, Alabama.

Uncle Daniel also prepared a second Certificate for the ceremony. He presented Grandmother with a Certificate in recognition of "Patience and Self Control."

It was a very proud day in Jimmy's life, but both recipients richly deserved the awards which they received.

CHAPTER SEVEN
CLEAN BATHE

Uncle Mark says:

Jimmy knew how to use the "key-mode." He didn't mess around about it either. When Jimmy said "key-mode," you found one for him, and quickly, too.

One time I took Jimmy out to eat. We went to that little catfish restaurant north of town. I don't know if it is still there. We were sitting at the table when Jimmy says "key-mode." I knew he meant business and I took him straight to the bathroom.

Well, it was one of those one bay jobs with a sink - not enough room for two people. So I sent Jimmy in, told him to lock the door, and stood outside the door to wait for him. I could tell from the sounds in the bathroom that Jimmy didn't say "key-mode" any too soon. It wasn't going to be any short visit to the key-mode. After awhile, Jimmy starts humming to himself. Then I hear the pig sounds for awhile. Then the horse clopping down the street.

Well, a little bit after Jimmy went in, another man came over to use the bathroom. He's standing there listening to these sounds wondering what in the world is going on in there. I kind of tried to look disinterested, like pig and horse sounds are common in restaurant bathrooms. I guess the guy figured I was standing in line, because he waited behind me all this time.

After an extended period, Jimmy finally finishes his business. From the sound of the flushing, I could tell that the "key-mode" was struggling to handle the large volume of material that Jimmy had just deposited into it. And when Jimmy opened that door and stuck his head out- Man alive! - a wall of fumes just hit me. It almost made me stagger. Gosh, it was thick in there.

I turned to the man who had been patiently waiting next to me. I smiled my most ingratiating smile. "Well, sir," I said motioning to the bathroom as invitingly as I could with my hand. "It's all yours."

For Jimmy, hygiene was a challenge. One reason was that Jimmy hated to take baths. Jimmy didn't see much reason why people took baths. So, after a few days without a bath, he didn't understand why so many other people were urging him to take a bath.

Jimmy took the world's fastest bath. Jimmy called it "clean bathe." When he was told to take a bath, Jimmy went into the bathroom with a change of clothing. After a short time, he emerged from the bathroom with his clothing changed. There was a problem with the "bath" though. You never heard any water running.

Once Grandaddy got wise to the waterless bath, he told Jimmy, "Jimmy, it is time to take your bath. And I want to hear some water running."

So Jimmy dutifully took his clothes into the bathroom. A little later, we heard some water running. After the "bath," however, you couldn't really discern any hygienic impact. We began to realize after a few such baths that, although we could hear water running, we couldn't hear any water splashing.

Jimmy's odor got so bad at one point, that Sharon, his beloved niece, instructed her husband, Mike, to talk Jimmy through a bath. Poor Mike stood outside the bathroom door and told Jimmy to run his water. He then made sure that he heard Jimmy get into the bathtub and that there were sufficient sounds of splashing. Next, Mike listed each body part as Jimmy washed, soaped and rinsed. Jimmy would not have taken a bath like that for just anyone, but he was willing to do it for Sharon. Likewise, I am not sure that Mike would have talked many people through a bath like that, but he was willing to do it for Sharon as well.

Jimmy was known for scratching where it itched when it itched. The scratch was far more important than the setting. He scratched in private and he scratched in public. Often, the scratch produced something interesting. Jimmy would pull his hand out, hold his finger up to the light, and inspect what the scratch had produced.

One Thanksgiving, Sharon's husband, Mike, forgot to pack a pair of long pants. Mike approached me and asked me if I had an extra pair of trousers that would fit him. He wore a different size of pants than I did, but I had a pair of sweatpants that I offered to him. At that point, Sharon came in. She told Mike that Jimmy had an extra pair of pants and that he could wear Jimmy's pants. I said, "Mike, you know that if you wear Jimmy's pants, you will end up scratching yourself just the way that Jim does. That clothing's got the 'cooties.'"

Mike laughed and said, "I think I can wear Jim's pants."

Mike went into the bathroom and put on Jimmy's pants. Within about ten minutes, Mike sidled up to me and quietly asked, "David, can I still borrow your sweat pants?"

"Sure, Mike" I replied. "Um...why do you want to wear my pants now?"

He looked at me sheepishly. "I know this sounds crazy, but I am beginning to itch something serious. I've got to change pants!"

Like all of us Jimmy loved to be pampered. He usually shaved himself, which meant that he usually had little tufts of hair or patches of whiskers on his face that he had missed while shaving.

When I visited, I would offer to shave Jim. His normal response was "*You doe 'head.*"

I ran water in the sink in the bathroom and got the shaving cream out of the cabinet. I then dampened Jimmy's face and spread the shaving cream on his face. Jim liked to look in the mirror with shaving cream all over his face. He pointed to his face and through the shaving cream said *"Brudder Bill"* (Brother Bill). Bill (my father) had grown a long, white beard. The beard fascinated Jimmy, and he liked to imagine himself with a white beard.

Next, I began shaving Jimmy. His whiskers were like steel wool. It didn't take many shaves for Jimmy's razors to become dull. His whiskers were particularly thick and wiry on his upper and lower lips. I had to get Jimmy to extend his chin and to stretch his lips in order to make any headway with those whiskers.

After the shave, I ran some warm water and soaked a wash cloth in it. I put the wash cloth over Jimmy's face like in a barbershop. Jimmy made "Oooo" sounds as if the wash cloth were too hot. As I wiped off his face with a wash cloth, Jimmy stuck that elongated tongue out through it. This protrusion initiated a game of "cat and mouse" in which I tried to grab his tongue through the wash cloth. Jimmy's massive tongue was probably stronger than my grip because I never could hang onto it for long when I grabbed it.

After the wash cloth treatment, I asked Jimmy if he had some aftershave. Jimmy always had aftershave because he regularly received it as a present. The family figured that anything they could give Jimmy to help with hygiene, or at least anything that they could give to help Jimmy cover his hygienic problems, was good. I applied aftershave liberally and told Jimmy that he smelled great.

Jimmy then reached into his pocket and produced a comb. I wet down his hair and then combed it. Jimmy didn't seem to mind it when I told him that he looked extremely handsome and that the ladies would love him.

I slicked back Jimmy's black hair much like a '50's hair style. Jimmy was a short person. If he was over five feet tall, it was not by much. With the slicked back hair, he looked for all the world like Squiggy from the television sitcom, *Laverne and Shirley*. Sharon's husband, Mike, began calling him Squiggy - or "Squiggs" for short.

Sharon also used her close relationship with Jimmy to try to help him with his hygiene. Sharon gave Jimmy an ear cleaning and manicure almost every time she visited Alabama. Sharon led Jim into the kitchen and he put his head down on the dining room table. Sharon filled a large bowl with warm water, and put a towel around Jimmy's ear. She used Q-tips - lots of Q-tips.

Sharon began probing in Jimmy's ear. Jimmy scrunched up his face tightly. Sharon asked, "Jimmy, are you okay, Honey?"

Through clenched teeth, and an expression that screamed "NO!" Jimmy compliantly replied "Uh-huh."

Sharon encouraged him, "You are doing great, Honey." Jimmy barely nodded his head.

Q-tip after loaded Q-tip came out of Jimmy's ear. Jimmy was a man who had a lot of superlatives. Based on what Sharon would dig out of his ear, he must have led central Alabama in ear wax production for a number of years.

Sharon then did a little irrigation with the water. When she was through, Jimmy's face had a huge look of relief - until he realized he still had another ear to go.

After the second ear, Sharon proceeded with a pedicure and a manicure. Trying to cut Jimmy's toe nails was a daunting task. Jimmy's toe nails were thicker than aluminum siding, and they seemed to be a whole lot stronger. Even soaking those nails didn't appear to do much good. Each clip was a loud "Crack!" After each clip, Jimmy grunted "Uh."

Then Sharon tried to clean out from under his fingernails. This cleaning was also difficult. Dirt and matter tended to cake under Jimmy's nails. For Sharon, it was a labor of love.

During a visit in Thanksgiving of 1997, Sharon decided that she needed some relief from the manicure and pedicure business. She resolved to take Jim for a professional job.

That Thanksgiving, Uncle Thomas, who worked for the Winn Dixie supermarket chain, brought some old Winn Dixie vests for his nephews. One vest said "Produce Manager," and another vest said "Customer Service Manager." Sharon's sons decided that they would wear the vests when they took Jimmy for his manicure. Jimmy wore a blue Winn Dixie vest that said "Location Manager."

Sharon took Jimmy to a nail boutique at a local shopping mall. The boutique was staffed by southeast Asian ladies who were not quite fluent in English. When Jimmy sat down in the manicure chair, he looked distinguished in his vest. During the whole manicure, the young Vietnamese manicurist looked up at Jimmy's vest, then at Jimmy's face, then over at Sharon, then back to Jimmy's nails. She turned and said something to her coworkers in her native tongue. She had the most perplexed look on her face, as if she couldn't decide whether her client was a big grocery store executive, or if her coworkers were playing a practical joke on her.

Uncle Mark says:

You just never knew what Jimmy was going to say. But he always seemed to know just what to say in every situation. I don't know if he ever missed a trick.

We were in a restaurant one day when Jimmy needs to go "key-mode." I knew not to fool around when he said "key-mode," so we went directly to the bathroom. It was a bathroom with stalls as well as a urinal on the wall next to the stalls. Jimmy went right for one of the stalls and starts his business. I stood outside the stall waiting for him to finish.

Well, in comes kind of a shady looking guy. He's got a raincoat on with the collar pulled up. He's a nervous type of guy with a furtive look on his face, and he's looking around a little anxiously as he heads for a urinal. I kind of half waved, half nodded at him as I leaned against Jimmy's stall waiting for Jimmy to finish. The man gives me a sideways, suspicious look through squinting eyes. I tried to look as inconspicuous as you can when you're standing alone beside an occupied stall in the men's bathroom for no apparent reason.

Then, Jimmy starts doing the pig sound in the stall. The guy at the urinal jerks his head up and glances over at the stall. He's wondering what in the world that sound is. He stares at Jimmy's stall and then he looks back at me. I can tell he's getting more nervous by the moment.

So I decided to try to assure him that nothing funny was going on. I kind of turn my head toward Jimmy's stall and say, "Everything okay in there, Jimmy?" I tried to smile at the stranger and to nod my head reassuringly.

At that point Jimmy stops making the pig sound. Jimmy sighs a long, lilting sigh. Then in that special, tender Jimmy tone, Jimmy says "Love you, John Mark."

Well, that man's eyes got as big as saucers. He shot out of the bathroom as fast as he could go. Jimmy and I kind of took our time in the bathroom. When we finally returned to the restaurant, we didn't see that guy anywhere. He was long gone.

"Brudder Bill!"

CHAPTER EIGHT
NO ME FALL DOWN

We were sitting at the breakfast table in Alabama one day. My brother, Arthur, had come down with us to visit Grandaddy and Grandmother. At breakfast, Grandaddy announced that he had decided to cut down some large trees around the garden. The trees cast too much shade on his garden plants. Grandaddy often saved large projects for visits from family members when he had someone to help him. Arthur and I were more than willing to oblige him.

Jimmy, however, was not the most enthusiastic person about work. If Grandaddy announced a project or some work that he wanted to do that day, and said, "Jimmy, you need to help us too," Jimmy's reaction was not necessarily positive. Frequently he slowly shook his head back and forth in silent dissent, or, as on this occasion, he expressed some indignation, "*Ugh!*"

Grandaddy said, "Now Jimmy, you need to be careful. You might get in a little trouble." Upon hearing the tone of Grandaddy's warning, Jimmy straightened up and stopped any fussing.

When we left the breakfast table, Jimmy headed to his room to get ready to go outside. He came over to me. He shook his head and whispered, "*Davy, no lite twouble. Weal HATE twouble.*"

A little later, Arthur, Jimmy and I were standing at the edge of the garden watching Grandaddy attempt to cut down a large tree with his chain saw. Jimmy was never a very willing participant in work, but he had been impressed into this work crew. Just because he had been drafted, however, did not mean he would use his maximum effort.

As Grandaddy sawed, he went a little too deep into the downhill side of the tree. The weight of the tree pressed down on the cut, closed in on the chain saw, and bound the blade. Grandaddy unsuccessfully tried to pull out the chain saw. He wiggled it. Then he yanked it. He couldn't extract it. The chain saw was stuck.

Grandaddy went and got a rope and a ladder. He put the ladder against the tree and climbed up. He tied the rope as high on the tree as he could. The plan was for Arthur, Jimmy and me to pull the upper part of the tree off of the chain saw from the uphill side, allowing Grandaddy to extract the saw from the cut.

The three of us grabbed hold of the rope. I was in front. Arthur was behind me, and Jimmy was behind Arthur. We gave a few tugs, but the tree would not budge.

"Okay, guys," I said. "We're really going to need to dig in on this one and pull in unison. When I say 'One...two...three...Tug,' then you pull with everything you got. Do you understand, Jim? When I say 'Tug!,' then you pull real hard. Okay?"

Jimmy shook his head. "*Yeah unnertan*" he said.

"Okay, Jimmy. Now pull hard."

Arthur and I dug in to pull with Jimmy behind us. I counted to three and shouted "Tug!" Arthur and I pulled with everything we had. What we didn't know was that Grandaddy had previously spliced this rope. Grandaddy was a survivor of the great Depression. He used a number of methods to extend the life of his possessions. Splicing a rope back together that was broken or frayed was one of his many tricks.

When we tugged, the rope went taut, and then burst apart at the splice. Arthur and I went flying backwards to the ground in a heap. As I began to scrape myself up off the ground, I turned and looked behind me to see if everyone was okay. Arthur was sitting on the ground, brushing himself off. Behind Arthur, there was Jimmy, still standing up. He had a nonchalant posture, and held the slackened end of the rope loosely with one hand. Jimmy stared down at Arthur and me crumpled on the ground. With a look of puzzlement on his face, he said *"No me fall down."*

Arthur and I were speechless. Jimmy shook his head slowly. With a tone of disgust, he repeated, *"No ME fall down."*

Jimmy's effort at the work site was not vigorous. Jimmy wasn't going to win many "atta boy" awards. He acted as if his goal was to expend as little energy as possible on a project. He distanced himself from the center of activity, and stood and watched others do the work as much as possible. One time, Grandaddy and I joked that Jimmy should work on a road side construction crew. We would buy him a shovel, and he could lean on it all day long watching the work.

The Alabama summers were very hot. Sometimes when we were working, we sent Jimmy to the house to get some water. The problem was that when we sent Jimmy into the house for water, he disappeared for an extended period. Getting water must have been a difficult task, because it often took Jimmy twenty or thirty minutes to reemerge with it.

On one occasion, we had been working for only fifteen or twenty minutes outside. Jimmy said, *"Need watta."*

Grandaddy said, "Well Jimmy, there is a hose. Turn it on and get some water."

Jimmy looked at Grandaddy and said, *"Need watta from houth."*

Grandaddy said, "Jimmy, if you need water, you can get it from the hose. You don't need to go to the house." Jimmy just shook his head in disgust. That was not the response that he wanted.

A few minutes later, Jimmy said, *"Need key-mode."*

Grandaddy was determined not to lose this battle. He responded, "Jimmy, there's a tree. Just step behind it and go right there." Jimmy shook his head again.

Jimmy paused. *"Need numma 2."*

Grandaddy looked at me kind of sideways. Jimmy had him there. For Jimmy, his relief efforts were described in terms of "Number 1" and "Number 2." You really didn't want to be around Jimmy when he needed to do "Number 2." He could relieve abdominal air pressure something fierce. Jimmy called it "bad gas." If somebody else such as myself broke wind, he said *"Davy bad gath."* When Jimmy did it, he said *"Bad gath"* and emitted a sigh of relief (*"Ahhh..."*) as if he had just done something very positive.

Grandaddy said, "Okay, Jimmy. You can go to the house." With a distinct look of triumph on his face, Jimmy walked to the house in his slow, ambling gait so he could do "Number 2." It must have been quite an effort too, because he didn't emerge from the house for a long time.

Jimmy did have regular assigned chores that he performed. Grandaddy and Grandmother believed that it was important for him to contribute as much as he could to the household. They also believed that it was important for him to have things that he could do. Jimmy cleaned his own room. He didn't like to be rushed though. More often than not, these room cleanings included an extensive review of pictures or of a cassette tape that he found during the cleaning. He would emerge from his room a number of times and say *"Lut Davy"* and show me a photograph, or play a portion of a cassette tape for me.

Jimmy took out the compost when it needed dumping. He went to the mail box twice a day - for the newspaper in the morning and for the mail in the afternoon. Another important assignment involved straightening the throw rugs in the hall. Grandaddy even marked a yard stick so that Jimmy could make sure that the walking rugs were the correct distance from the wall.

Jimmy also helped with the laundry. Before Grandmother had a dryer, he carried the laundry basket for her to the clothesline and held it while she hung the laundry to dry. He tactfully looked away when she hung something indelicate like a lady's undergarment. When the laundry was dry, Jimmy carried the basket outside and took down the laundry.

In the kitchen, Jimmy helped set the table. After supper, he helped do the dishes.

Doing dishes with Jimmy was an interesting experience. Jimmy preferred to dry the dishes. Washing the dishes required too much work. Jimmy was probably better suited to drying anyway, since his dish washing was not the most thorough in the world.

The problem with Jimmy drying the dishes was that he was not very fast. He loved to talk. He asked you if you remembered so and so, or remembered such and such. He reviewed the same subjects over and over again. Since he was talking while you were washing, the dish drainer gradually filled up until there wasn't any place to put the dishes that you were washing. Encouraging Jimmy to speed up was not very effective. He was focused more on talking than on drying.

One time, I thought of a plan to try to speed him up. Knowing how competitive Jimmy was, I said, "Jimmy, it doesn't matter how fast you dry, you can't beat me. I am going to finish washing these dishes before you finish drying them."

Jimmy immediately began to dry vigorously. He said, "*Me beat you. Now you learn.*"

Jimmy tackled his stack of dishes and sure enough, he began to catch up. No matter how fast he dried though, I was getting each dish washed before he could dry it. "Jimmy", I said, "I am going to beat you."

As I got near the end of the dish washing, Jimmy began to understand what was happening. I turned to say something to Grandmother. When I turned back, the plate in my dish water looked familiar. I washed the dish and put it into the dish drainer.

A minute later, the same dish reappeared in my dish water. I heard a little snicker. Jimmy said, "*Need wash dish Davy.*" He snickered again.

"Jimmy," I said, "if you keep this up, then we will never finish washing the dishes." Eventually, the dish replacement stopped, and Jimmy never did find a way to beat me washing the dishes.

Uncle Stephen says:

Working with that Jimmy could be a challenge. One day Papa needed help putting up a board with some screws in it. He needed some one to hold the board up while he screwed it in. Jimmy was the only one there to help him that day, so he got Jimmy to hold up the board.

As Jimmy was holding up the board, Papa said to him, "Now, Jimmy, don't let go." I don't know if Jimmy didn't understand him or what. He might have thought that Papa said to let go. Anyway, Jimmy immediately let go of the board. It came crashing down and one of the screws gouged Papa in his hand. It got him pretty good too.

We were sitting at the breakfast table in Alabama one day. My brother, Michael, had come down with us to visit Grandaddy and Grandmother. At breakfast, Grandaddy announced that he had decided to cut down a large pine tree behind the house that was dying. He was concerned that it would fall on the house if a strong wind blew it down.

Grandaddy had thought about it awhile. He couldn't fell the tree backwards away from the house because it would land in his garden. On the left side of the tree was a steep bank that was almost impossible to negotiate. On the right side of the tree was the unpaved driveway for about 25 yards, and then another steep bank. At the bottom of that hill was a collection of three or four automobiles that had once been operable. They were now rusted shells.

Grandaddy decided his only option was to tie a rope as high on the tree as he could, and for his "work crew" to pull the tree to the right side of the house while he cut the tree with his chain saw. The work crew on this day was me, Michael, and a reluctant Jimmy. As Grandaddy explained his plan to us, it did occur to us that he was asking us to pull the tree in such a way that it would land on the very spot from which we were pulling. We expressed our safety concerns to Grandaddy, but he insisted we could pull the rope and then beat a hasty retreat before any harm befell us.

Grandaddy climbed up the tree and placed the rope (which I inspected to insure that it had not been spliced) around the tree as high as he could. I pulled the work crew together to coordinate our plan. "Listen, guys" I said. "I'm going to say 'Pull,' and then we all pull in unison. Each time I say 'Pull,' then we pull. When that tree starts to fall, I'm going to yell 'Run!' When I yell 'Run!,' drop the rope and run as hard as you can away from the house."

I looked at Jimmy who didn't say anything. "Do you understand, Jimmy? When I say 'Pull,' you pull. When I say 'Run!,' you run that way." I pointed to the cars at the bottom of the hill.

Jimmy said "*Yeah unnertan.*"

We got on the end of the rope. I was in front, Michael was behind me, and Jimmy was behind him. Grandaddy cranked up the chain saw and started cutting. When Grandaddy had cut deep enough, he motioned for us to start pulling.

"Pull!" I yelled and we started pulling the tree toward us. I focused carefully on the top of the tree to see when it began to move.

"Pull!" I yelled again. We pulled. No movement. The saw kept cutting.

"Pull!" I yelled. We pulled. No movement.

The fourth time I yelled "Pull!" I heard a familiar crack of wood. The top of the tree began to plummet toward us.

"Run!" I yelled. "Run!" As I turned to run, I noticed that Michael was right beside me. Jimmy, however, was not. I raised my head to look farther. Jimmy was across the driveway, down the hill, and in the middle of the rusted cars, running as hard as he could. He was digging for everything he had.

I let out a guffaw and almost tripped and fell. Michael and I scrambled away and a couple of seconds later the pine tree landed right where we had been standing. The house was unharmed - to Grandaddy's great satisfaction.

Jimmy later proclaimed that it had been an extremely difficult job. "*Whew!*" he said, shaking his head at the difficulty. "*Hard job!*" We questioned Jimmy to try to determine at what point he actually began running, but we never got a clear answer.

Later I told Michael "That Jimmy must be the fastest man on earth."

Michael and I laughed. I paused for a moment, then I added, "Or the most shrewd."

Michael laughed again, but not quite as hard as before.

CHAPTER NINE
FELLA AND LADY

I loved to visit Alabama. The welcome alone made a person happy that he came. When I called to say I was coming to visit, there was obvious joy in the voice at the other end of the telephone. If I expressed that the arrival time might be uncertain, Grandmother said, "We will look for you when we see you." She meant it. Whatever time you did arrive, you didn't have to go knock on the front door or ring a doorbell. Even if you arrived late at night, Grandaddy, Grandmother and Jimmy came out of the house and greeted you at your car with smiles and hugs. They were happy to see you and it showed.

After we arrived, we proceeded into the house and sat down in the living room. Whatever Grandaddy and Grandmother had been doing stopped. They focused their attention on the visitor as we caught up on news. Sometimes this welcoming conversation lasted for hours.

If you arrived before supper (which we normally tried to do), Grandmother prepared one of your favorite meals. Grandmother kept track of the meals that each person liked. Pleasing others was important to Meme, and she went to great pains to do so. In my case, she cooked pot roast, potatoes, gravy, and her homemade whole wheat rolls. Those rolls melted in your mouth. Jimmy loved this meal, too. We always laughed when Jimmy appreciatively smacked his lips and said, "*Mm-mm. Duud roach! DUUD roach!*" (Good roast).

Grandmother and Grandaddy understood hospitality, and they had a vision for family. This vision was their focus and their passion. It was the guidepost of their lives, and it was one reason children, grandchildren, great-grandchildren and in-laws received such a warm welcome at the home place in Wetumpka, Alabama.

Grandmother had contracted rheumatic (scarlet) fever when she was a child. She suffered a series of attacks beginning in the 4th grade. Each attack weakened her more, and left her bedridden for weeks. Finally, the doctor told her mother that Grandmother would die within a matter of days. Out of desperation, her mother moved the family to a drier climate in Lubbock, Texas. Grandmother wondrously recovered.

Although she survived the rheumatic fever, the doctors told Grandmother that the illness left scar tissue on her heart. She was warned that pregnancy and particularly child birth would be life threatening events for her. This threat did not deter her from pursuing her vision for family. One of my uncles told me that he calculated that Meme had a child two years of age or under in the home for 17 straight years! During 10 of those years, she cared for **two** children two years of age or under.

Grandmother and Grandaddy were careful to communicate their vision for family to us. Numerous family pictures graced the living room. In the hallway hung a drawing of a family tree which showed the branches of their family with each member. Every time a new grandchild or great-grandchild was born, a new line was added to a branch of the tree.

Grandmother and Granddaddy communicated their vision verbally, but they communicated it even more powerfully by their example. We were all beneficiaries of the vision for family. Jimmy was a beneficiary as well.

Yet Grandaddy's and Grandmother's hospitality extended beyond family. It was an expression of their faith. Through their lives, they opened their hearts and their home to other needy persons, not just family. Joe, Catherine, Mike, and Dave - there were a number of persons that received encouragement, succor, and a roof over their heads from Papa and Meme when they had no other place to call home.

Catherine R. was one of those less fortunate souls who was blessed to encounter Papa and Meme. Catherine said her husband left her. He then divorced her. She began a downward spiral emotionally and financially and, in the process, became alienated from her family. She had almost no friends and she was destitute when Papa and Meme opened their home to her.

It wasn't that Catherine was an unfriendly or antisocial person. In fact, she was too friendly. She tried to help in any way that she could, almost throwing herself at you. Catherine had such a need for belonging...such a craving for acceptance that she tried way too hard to be helpful. She smothered other people with herself. It was almost repulsive. Jimmy certainly was not her Number One fan. When Catherine sensed a rejection of her good intentions from other people, it only injured her esteem more. Catherine was a wounded soul. But Meme specialized in wounded souls.

Meme took Catherine under her wing. She knew that Catherine needed to be busy and to do things that she could feel good about. Meme put Catherine to work cooking, cleaning, sewing and baking. Meme worked with her and praised her successes. During the next few months, Meme encouraged Catherine, listened to her, and counseled her. Meme prayed for her, and Meme prayed with her, sharing the love of God tangibly and intangibly.

Catherine's personal esteem slowly grew. Her self-destructive habits began to diminish. She received balm for her wounds and hope for her future. Catherine recovered to the extent that she was able to move out and live on her own. Yet she knew that if she needed support or a listening ear at any time, she had a friend in Meme that was faithful, caring and available.

Grandmother prominently displayed a framed statement in her room that inspired her. It also described her perspective. The statement read:

PEOPLE NEED LOVING THE MOST
WHEN THEY DESERVE IT THE LEAST

And it wasn't as if Papa and Meme had a lot of room. In the mid-1960's, while they still lived at the Narrow Lane Road house, Grandaddy found some very inexpensive land north of Montgomery in Elmore County, Alabama. The land was located on a dirt and gravel road, about four miles off of any paved road. The area was full of red clay and scrub pine common to the rural Deep South. Wetumpka was the closest town. With help from his sons, Grandaddy built a brick house at the top of a hill. This house had four bedrooms and two baths. Jimmy called this house the *"bwick houth,"* or in later years, the *"ol' houth top of hill."*

After most of the Martin children had left home in the early 1970's, Grandaddy, again with assistance from his family, built a smaller house about a quarter mile down the road from the "brick house." Jimmy called this house the *"lil' houth"* because it was smaller. It initially had only three bedrooms and one bath, with a basement.

Over time, Grandaddy added another room to the little house, and he furnished the basement. Whether they had a lot of room or a little room, Grandaddy and Grandmother welcomed scores of people- a number of them less fortunate souls. If they had limited room, they simply made do.

Jimmy liked the "little house" though. It was the first house at which he had a room that was all his own. Jimmy's room was not large at all. In fact, it was pretty small. Two people could barely turn around in it. But Jimmy loved having a room that he could call his own.

In his room, he had a bed, a small desk, a closet, and a little bedside table. Almost every time I visited Alabama, Jimmy wanted to rearrange the furniture in his room. He would say *"Need bed unna window"* or *"Need bed on wall."* We then had to help Jimmy move each piece of furniture until it was positioned exactly where he wanted it. More than once I pointed out to him that we were simply moving his furniture back to the same place it occupied before we had rearranged it on the last visit.

Jimmy's need to reconfigure his furniture regularly was somewhat baffling. Maybe he had a sense of interior design that required fulfillment. Maybe his decor was one thing that he actually could control and it made him feel secure to exercise that control. In any event, he insisted that it had to be done.

If Jimmy had feelings of insecurity, those feelings were certainly understandable. He had gone from pillar to post before coming to live with the Martin family. While with the Martin family, he still knew that he had another family. Jimmy used to say, *"Got two fadder. Got two mudder. Got two sister and lotsa, lotsa brudder."*

When he was about thirty years old though, Jimmy went through a rebellious stage. A feeling of detachment often occurs with adopted or foster children. Jimmy began to express dissatisfaction at home and to reject Papa and Meme. He told everyone that Grandmother and Grandaddy were not his "real parents." Jimmy had previously called Grandaddy and Grandmother either "Daddy" or "Mama," or their names of affection, "Papa" and "Meme."

For a number of months, however, Jimmy began to call Grandaddy and Grandmother – "Fella" and "Lady." He said, *"Not my weal Momma and Daddy."*

For years, Jimmy had an occasional visit at the house of his "real" grandmother. Myrtle Johnson was Jimmy's maternal grandmother. Jimmy just called her "Mer." Unlike Grandmother and Grandaddy, Mer had a television and other coveted forms of entertainment. Jimmy was allowed to sit in front of the television at Mer's house for hours on end. He was otherwise spoiled and indulged. He loved it. As often happens to children who are spoiled by their grandparents, Jimmy resented the fact that he was not accorded the same levels of indulgence and entertainment when he returned home.

Jimmy's "Fella and Lady" stage lasted for a number of months. Jimmy proclaimed that he was going to go live with his "real" family.

When we visited Jimmy, he told us that Grandmother and Grandaddy were not his "real parents." We tried to appeal to our relationship. "Jimmy," I said. "What about your brothers and sisters, aren't they your brothers and sisters?"

Jimmy would have none of it. *"Yeah lub brudder sister. Not my WEAL Momma and Daddy."* His resentment ran deep.

During this time, Grandaddy and Grandmother were patient with Jimmy. Like most parents with rebellious children, they were saddened by their child's rejection. They knew, though, that they could not change their child's heart. Grandaddy and Grandmother gave each other support during this time and continued to parent and show Jimmy love to the extent he was willing to receive it. They had to trust that they had established a relational foundation with Jimmy over the years that would survive this stage. Hopefully, Jimmy would grow out of the rebellion, or something would happen that would change Jimmy's attitude.

And something did happen that changed Jimmy's heart. No one knows the exact details. Jimmy went on one of his visits to Mer's house. A blow up of some type occurred and unpleasantries were exchanged. Most likely Jimmy drove his grandmother to distraction and she lost control. The incident scared Jimmy.

When Jimmy came back home from that visit, "Fella and Lady" completely disappeared.   Jimmy did not visit his grandmother again. From that point on, it was "Daddy" and "Mama" or "Papa" and "Meme." Jimmy would say, *"Weal nithe Papa tate* (take) *me. Mate my fadda happy. Make my mudda happy. Weal nithe him tate me."*

The Martin family was Jimmy's family...permanently.

CHAPTER TEN
1-2-3-4-5

Jimmy and I were riding in the car with Uncle Tim one day. A few raindrops began to fall and Uncle Tim turned on his windshield wipers. We talked for awhile about family. Jimmy then held his right hand out vertically in front of his face, and started moving it up and down as if he were waving away a fly.

I watched him for a little bit, wondering what in the world he was doing.

"Jimmy," I asked. "are you moving your arm like a windshield wiper?"

Jimmy continued doing the motion. "Baby sister" is all he said as he did it. "Baby sister" was a pet name for Aunt Rebecca, particularly used by Uncle Tim.

"Tim, what is he doing?" I asked.

Uncle Tim shook his head. "Well, David, I don't think anybody really knows. He's been doing this motion for awhile, but I don't think anyone has quite figured out what it is."

Jimmy kept waving his hand.

"Jimmy, is it like the windshield wipers?" I asked.

Jimmy didn't contradict me, and I decided that was the best guess we had. Yet I didn't really think we understood exactly what he was doing.

On my next visit to Alabama a few months later, I was talking with Uncle Tim. He said, "David, you remember that motion that Jimmy was making with his hand?"

"Yes I remember" I replied.

"Well, I think we figured out what it is."

Tim showed me a family videotape that he had made. The tape was made in the front yard of the "little house." Tim focused the camera on Aunt Rebecca at one point and she waved her hand back and forth in front of her face as if to say "Please get that camera off of me."

Jimmy had seen the videotape. He was fascinated by Aunt Rebecca's reaction to the camera and was imitating her. Of course, no one blamed Aunt Rebecca if she had an aversion to cameras.

Grandmother and Grandaddy did not own a television throughout their entire lives. Grandaddy said that a television brought bad news and bad images into his house and that he did not need bad news or bad images.

Jimmy loved television. He loved movies. When we visited someone else's home, he sat in front of the television for hours at a time - simply mesmerized. Movies affected Jimmy. One did not have to look much further than Jimmy to reinforce the argument that what we see influences our behavior.

One time, at Uncle Stephen's house, we watched the Civil War movie, *The Horse Soldiers*, starring the Duke himself, John Wayne. In *The Horse Soldiers,* John Wayne leads his Union cavalry on a raid through the South, antagonizing men, women and animals along the way. For days after that movie, Jimmy marched around the house like a soldier. He stopped, saluted some one, and then marched around some more, barking orders to an imaginary corps like the Duke. (I guess we should be thankful he wasn't kicking things around as well).

Later on, Uncle Daniel gave Grandmother and Grandaddy a VCR with a monitor. With the VCR, Jimmy could watch shows on videotape that were approved by Grandmother and Grandaddy. Every evening before he went to bed, Jimmy had *"bwake time."* Break time consisted of a bowl of ice cream, a drink, and a videotape. Jimmy didn't call it a "videotape." He called it *"rado fill."* The "radio film" at break time was usually two *Gospel Bill* shows. *Gospel Bill* is an episodic children's western set in a rural Midwestern town. The sheriff of that town, Gospel Bill, is surrounded by an assortment of peculiar characters, including his bumbling deputy, Nicodemus.

As Jimmy watched Gospel Bill have a shoot out, Jimmy slowly raised his hand - thumb up in the air and forefinger extended like a pistol. When Jimmy "shot" his finger pistol, he didn't say "Bang!" or "Kapow!" His shots sounded more like "*Pew-pew! Pew-pew!*"

When Jimmy had an audience, his dramatizations were not performed quickly. Everything was enacted in slow motion for effect. The arm with the hand pistol was raised slowly, and Jimmy took aim deliberately. The shot was directed and targeted. This idea of slow motion probably came from the sports phenomenon of instant replay. Jimmy had seen enough football games in which great plays were replayed in slow motion. Jimmy was just creating some highlights of his own.

When we visited Jimmy, we would try to take him out for a meal and a movie as a special treat. Jimmy loved to go out. It was a break from the hum drum of his everyday life, and it was a chance for Jimmy to socialize. On one occasion, we took him to see the children's movie, *Cats and Dogs*. In that movie, cats and dogs have human traits and wage battle against the other species in a tale of comedic espionage. The animals talk to each other using sophisticated equipment like computers, walkie talkies, and phones. After about twenty or thirty minutes of animal intrigue, Jimmy turned to me with the most skeptical look on his face. He whispered in an incredulous tone, "*Davy, dog tan't talt!?!*" (Dogs can't talk!). Based on what he was witnessing at the time though, he didn't sound real sure.

Another time, we took Jimmy to see the remake of the movie *Flubber*. In *Flubber*, a scientist invents an antigravity material which has the consistency of rubber. At one point in the movie, the scientist puts Flubber into his car and drives it in the sky like some type of alien spaceship. Jimmy turned to me in the theater and said, "*Hey! Tar way up!*"(Car way up!). For years after that, Jimmy would shake his head incredulously and look at me and say "*Davy, tar way up!*" For Jimmy, movies were kind of a reality check.

Sometimes, Jimmy's love of entertainment got him into trouble. For a while, we noticed that he began locking his bedroom door at about 9:00 PM each evening. He often did not emerge until the next morning. When he did emerge, he was sleepy and grumpy.

Jimmy had found a radio band that picked up the audio from a Birmingham television station. As it turns out, Jimmy's favorite show was the western, *Gunsmoke*. Unfortunately for Jimmy, *Gunsmoke* was broadcast very late at night.

Grandaddy eventually discovered what was going on, and he decided that Jimmy shouldn't stay up into the wee hours of the morning listening to his Birmingham television station. For a long time, Jimmy was required to turn in his radio each night. Before Jimmy went to bed, he had to unplug his radio, go knock on Grandmother and Grandaddy's door, and turn it over to them so that he would not stay up and listen to it. This nightly routine caused Jimmy some chagrin, but he complied with it. Ultimately, Jimmy himself probably realized that it was not best for him to become addicted to late night television, or at least the closest equivalent available to him.

When Jimmy was about twenty years old, someone in the family got the idea that Jimmy might enjoy having a camera. Jimmy loved to look at pictures. He especially loved to see pictures of pretty girls. The idea of buying Jimmy a camera was a good one. Jimmy's camera became one of his prized possessions, rivaling the love of his tape players and radio. Jimmy could never have enough film for his camera. Shopping with Jimmy meant looking for tape players and film.

One of Jimmy's first subjects with his camera was Aunt Rebecca. At the time, Aunt Rebecca was in her bath robe with hair curlers in her hair. She probably thought that there was no way that Jimmy could operate the camera - much less take a picture. She agreed to pose for Jimmy and did so with a smirk on her face. To Rebecca's chagrin, the picture was crystal clear and centered perfectly. It showed Aunt Rebecca in all her salon glory. Jimmy enjoyed showing it often. It is still a legendary picture in the Martin family. Poor Aunt Rebecca has been a little camera shy ever since that picture.

Jimmy's first camera was a small portable one. He could snap pictures quickly with it. A few years later, a family member bought him a Polaroid Instant camera. With the Polaroid, the pictures developed immediately and Jimmy could see them on the spot. The problem with the Polaroid, however, was that the operator had to push the flash button in and hold it until a green light appeared beside a red light in order to take the picture. Jimmy did not understand the concept of red and green lights in the camera viewfinder. However, he was taught to count to "5" slowly out loud before taking the picture, so the camera would work properly. For this reason, Jimmy's Polaroid camera became known as his "1-2-3-4-5 camera."

If Aunt Rebecca had the notion that Jimmy couldn't operate a camera, it was a reasonable one. If you ever saw Jimmy operate a camera, you wondered how in the world he ever made any pictures. When Jimmy took a picture with his "1-2-3-4-5 camera," he put his right eye up to the view finder. He, however, did not close his left eye. He counted slowly, *"Ooone-twooo-fweee-foe-fieee."* During the count, Jimmy's head moved around in a circle, and the camera moved with it. His left eye - the eye that Jimmy's subjects saw - rolled around in his eye socket. A person wondered what his right eye was doing in the viewfinder. There was no way that he could be focused on any one object, or even remotely have anything framed.

At the moment Jimmy took the picture, however, the camera (and the roving eye) stopped moving and froze. To our amazement, his pictures were almost always well framed and beautifully taken.

Once, we – the picture subjects - decided to follow Jimmy's "roving eye." As Jimmy slowly counted to five, the whole group shuffled right, then left, then right again - following the movement of his left eye. Jimmy was unfazed and took a great picture anyway.

Not that anyone didn't get cut off from Jimmy's pictures. It wasn't unusual for a person to be on the edge of Jimmy's picture with only one-half of that person showing. I myself was cut off in a "Jimmy picture" a number of times. This phenomenon didn't happen because Jimmy was a bad photographer. This phenomenon happened because Jimmy focused on the object that HE wanted to photograph. This object was usually a pretty girl or a slick car or, if Jimmy was having a good day, it was both. A disproportionate number of Jim's pictures showed a beautiful young lady standing in front of a car. Many of those same pictures have a part of me or some other less favored subject cut off on the edge. Those of us who were not beautiful or who did not drive glamorous vehicles were simply not Jimmy's favorite subjects, and we often only got to see parts of ourselves in his pictures.

Jimmy usually wanted his picture to be taken as well. When another family member operated Jimmy's camera, that member counted slowly in Jimmy's manner, using the necessary language, "*Ooone-twooo-fweee-foe-fieee.*" It wasn't hard to get people to smile when you operated Jimmy's camera.

If you were looking through pictures with Jimmy and you came upon the picture of a pretty girl, which happened often, he often held the picture up and showed it to you. He then brought the picture up to his mouth. He did this slowly, extending his ample lips over the subject. He then placed a long, meaningful kiss on the photograph. During the kiss, Jimmy glanced over at you, smiling as much as a person can smile who has his lips puckered up to a photograph. He then put the picture down and said "She fall in love with me."

Jimmy's memory was phenomenal. Jimmy had photo albums, picture books, and boxes and boxes of pictures. To us, it seemed like he had hundreds of pictures in mass disarray. Jimmy, however, could mention a picture to you. If you didn't remember the picture, or expressed any hesitation regarding it, he went to his room, put his finger on it within a matter of seconds, and brought the picture back to show you exactly which one he was talking about.

The Martin family held a large family reunion every Thanksgiving. Jimmy called it "Big Turkey Day." One Thanksgiving in the late 1990's, Jimmy looked at Sharon's husband, Mike Freeman. Jimmy said, "Hey! Same shirt Big Turkey Day, 1992." We all kind of looked at each other as if to say "What is he talking about?" Jimmy went to his room and was back with the picture almost immediately. The picture showed Mike Freeman wearing the exact same shirt, and at the bottom of the photograph was written "Thanksgiving 1992."

In Jimmy, many people saw a grown man with the mind of a five year old - a simpleton. Some people had an attitude of disdain toward Jimmy. Jimmy, however, had talents.

Jimmy had a phenomenal memory. Grandmother had a great memory for names, dates and details. If, however, she couldn't remember a detail, she asked Jimmy. More often than not, Jimmy remembered what Grandmother could not. We could be discussing a memorable family event like my brother Daniel's "choo-choo" train birthday. When Daniel was young, Grandmother made him a "choo-choo" train cake for his birthday. If Grandmother didn't remember how many train cars were on that cake, she asked Jimmy and he would know.

But what was the source of Jimmy's photographic ability? He had no training with a camera. Yet he took great pictures beginning with his very first one. Eventually, we concluded that Jimmy had been blessed with a natural spatial talent. He instinctively framed his pictures. Like the regular rearrangement of the furniture in his room, his pictures evidenced an unusual aptitude for order and dimension. My respect for Jimmy's talents grew as I grew.

CHAPTER ELEVEN
LIKE SHARON BEST

Uncle Thomas says:
One Sunday afternoon another family from church came to visit us. The family had a father, a mother and a rather large teenage daughter. The purpose of the visit was a friendly social call - one of those "get to know you" visits.

The family came in the front door and greetings were exchanged. Jimmy was a young teenager then. He walked through the living room on the way to his room. Jimmy stopped and stared at the family. He looked at the father, the mother, and then the daughter. I am sure the family looked at him too. People often didn't know what to make of Jimmy when they saw him.

Jimmy surveyed the daughter from head to toe and he started shaking his head back and forth. He said "No like fat legs." To make sure he was heard, he again said "No LIKE fat legs." Jimmy then proceeded on to his room, as everyone else watched in stunned silence.

I don't think that family ever visited us again.

Jimmy was a study in contradiction. He was a social person to whom relationships were extremely important. Jimmy hated it when close relationships were broken and sought intently to heal those breaches. Yet at the same time, Jimmy had the childlike quality of saying exactly what was on his mind. He was what could only be described as outspoken. Jimmy meant to be diplomatic, but his forthright tongue often had the opposite effect.

I took my future bride, Mary Beth, to Alabama for the first time in 1981. It was the annual family reunion at Thanksgiving ("Big Turkey Day"). Mary Beth and I were not formally engaged, but I was quite serious about her at the time. For me to introduce her to all those family members, and especially to Jimmy, meant that I was serious about her.

Mary Beth and I rode to Alabama together with my sister, Sharon, and her husband, Mike Freeman. When we arrived, we got out of the car. Grandaddy, Grandmother and Jimmy came out to greet us. Jimmy walked up and looked at Mary Beth. He looked at Sharon; then back at Mary Beth. Jimmy blurted "Like Sharon best!" Thankfully, Grandmother and Grandaddy loved company. They warmly greeted Mary Beth and they received her with open arms.

That November night, after supper and a lot of family time, Grandaddy emptied the ashes from the wood stove and we went to bed. After I had been in bed about an hour, I was awakened to cries of "Fire! Fire!" Apparently, there were live coals in the ashes that Grandaddy had thrown into the woods behind the house. The coals ignited some dry leaves and the fire spread rapidly. We all ran outside and grabbed what we had available to fight the fire - shovels, rakes, brooms, mops, etc. Grandaddy tried to use the hose but we had a limited water supply because the water level in the well was low.

We all fought the fire as best we could, trying to keep it away from the house. I still have the image in my mind of Mary Beth in her Carolina blue velour robe wielding a broom and trying to beat out flames. I can't say that I decided to marry her at that moment, but that image certainly did not hurt the cause. After about an hour and a half of firefighting, we were able to extinguish the blaze and we all went inside to go to bed. For years after that, we teased Grandaddy that he wanted to make a big impression on Mary Beth, so he set the woods on fire.

The next morning, we got up for breakfast. No one could cook breakfast like Grandmother. It had its own special name. We called it a "Meme breakfast." She cooked eggs, bacon, sausage, gravy, and biscuits. The biscuits melted in your mouth and alone were good enough to make a meal. But Grandmother also had great things to put on the biscuits - treats like wild Muscadine grape jelly, blackberry jam, fig preserves, and pear preserves. There just wasn't anything quite like a Meme breakfast.

In addition, the breakfast included the one dish necessary to make it an Alabama breakfast - something local folk called "Alabama ice cream." No breakfast in Alabama was complete without grits. Grits flavored with butter and maybe a dash of salt. In fact, when I was in law school, I heard about a lawsuit that had been filed in the State of Alabama over some grits.

One time a patron in Alabama ordered breakfast in a local diner. The menu listed eggs, bacon, and toast, which is what the patron ordered. The waitress brought him eggs, bacon and toast. The patron asked "Where are my grits?"

The waitress said, "The menu says eggs, bacon, and toast, and that is what you got."

The patron said, "It isn't breakfast without grits." The restaurant, though, refused to serve him grits.

The patron was so chagrined that he took the restaurant to court. According to the story, an Alabama court issued a ruling that found that the word "breakfast" in the State of Alabama, by definition, includes grits.

Meme was a law abiding citizen. She understood the meaning of the word "breakfast." A "Meme breakfast" included grits.

That morning, Mary Beth sat down to eat her first Alabama breakfast. She served her plate, including grits. She asked for someone to pass the sugar. Mary Beth then began to sprinkle sugar on her grits. Mary Beth explained later that she sprinkled sugar on any "hot breakfast cereal." Grits in Alabama, however, are not a "hot breakfast cereal."

Jimmy tended to focus on pretty young girls like Mary Beth. As she began to sprinkle sugar on her grits, though, his eyes began to get bigger and bigger. He said, "*Whaaat?*"

At that moment, I realized what was happening. I was sitting across the table, however, and couldn't do anything about it. I really hoped that Jimmy would not draw everyone's attention to this obvious breach of Alabama etiquette.

"*Whaaat?*" Jimmy repeated. Then "*Sugah on gwits? Unh! No unnertan!*"

Mary Beth's face turned red. "*Sugah on gwits?*" Jimmy repeated and began to shake his head back and forth like it was the strangest thing he had ever seen.

Thankfully, Mary Beth was under the wing of Grandmother, who was one of the most gracious souls that God ever created. Grandmother said, "If Mary Beth wants to eat sugar on her grits, then she certainly can put sugar on her grits."

To Jimmy's consternation, Mary Beth ate her grits – sugar and all. It definitely left an impression on him. In future years, if Mary Beth spooned grits onto her plate at breakfast, Jimmy stopped eating, got up, grabbed the sugar bowl, and set it in front of Mary Beth's place.

One time when I visited Alabama, Grandmother and Grandaddy got sick. I did the best I could to take care of Jimmy. I dutifully got up in the morning to cook breakfast for Jimmy. I fixed eggs over easy, bacon, grits and toast. It wasn't a "Meme" breakfast, but not a bad job as breakfasts go.

Jimmy sat down to the table to eat. I served his plate and set it in front of him. Jimmy looked at it and began shaking his head. He muttered in disgust, *"Davy took won' edd."* Jimmy was used to eggs scrambled, not eggs over easy. I had cooked the "wrong egg" and Jimmy refused to eat it. I cooked more eggs, scrambling them this time. By the time Grandmother began to feel better the next day, I had a much stronger appreciation for everything that she did for Jimmy, and for what life without Meme would have been like.

I wasn't the only person unable to meet the standards set by "Meme breakfasts."

Rachel (my mother) says:

Jimmy is not a vegetarian! One time I made breakfast for Jimmy. I served him cereal with milk. When I set the bowl in front of Jimmy, he looked at it incredulously. Then he said "No lite cold food! Where da MEAT?!?"

Jimmy's table manners were not exactly exemplary. He loved food and he tended to wolf it down. For a long time, his favorite food was fried chicken. One day though, he ate so much chicken so fast, it made him vomit. After that episode, Grandaddy tried to monitor Jimmy's eating more closely. And Jimmy expressed a preference for hamburgers for a while.

The speed of Jimmy's eating led to some interesting sounds - slurping, smacking and swallowing - while the food was going down. After the food went down, it was not unusual for Jimmy to burp three or four times during a meal. These normally were not soft, muffled burps, but loud, coarse expressions of digestive reorganization. After each burp, Jimmy smiled and said, *"Theron belch!"*

Then after a pause – *"Tant you, Theron!"* - for good measure.

No one knows why Sharon's name was invoked with gratitude after a loud burp, except for the close kinship he felt with Sharon. But her name regularly was invoked unless Sharon was present. In that case, we heard the proper *"Oh! 'Tuse me!"* instead, which Sharon and her presence required.

On one of my many trips to Alabama, my mother, Rachel, sent some packages to the family. In one of these packages were some spicy toasted pecans that she had made.

Jimmy hated nuts. He didn't like peanuts or any other type of nut. He did, however, love his sister, Rachel. Rachel was the oldest child, and Jimmy affectionately called her his "big sister." When we put out the pecans and told Jimmy that they were from Rachel, he had a dilemma. Grandaddy teasingly said, "Jimmy, Rachel sent these pecans to us. Why don't you try one?"

Jimmy hesitated. Grandaddy said, "Jimmy, go ahead. Rachel made these just for us."

Jimmy slowly reached out and gingerly picked up a pecan. He stared at it between his fingers with a look of disgust. Then he looked at us. We gave him encouraging, expectant looks and he slowly put it into his mouth and began chewing.

Jimmy's face immediately scrunched up like he had just bit into a lemon. He was obviously not enjoying that pecan. Grandaddy said "Jimmy, do you like it?"

Although Jimmy's whole expression said "Yuck!" he nodded his head up and down affirmatively and said *"Uh-huh."*

Grandaddy smiled and asked, "Since you like it, do you want another one?"

Jimmy vigorously shook his head back and forth sideways and said *"Unh-unh."*

"Are they good?"

"*Uh-huh. Yeah lite.*"

"Don't you want another one?"

"*You doe 'head.*" Jimmy had done his duty and he wasn't about to touch another pecan.

Jimmy was a man that was willing to go to great lengths for love, but even he had his limits.

Diplomacy was fine and good. When he wished, Jimmy could compete with the most diplomatic. There were, however, some social mistakes that were not forgivable.

One day, we were sitting around the dinning room table discussing friends of the family. Grandaddy said, "Jimmy, how about Betty Hubbard?"

Jimmy immediately began shaking his head from side to side and waving his hand back and forth in front of his face. Jimmy clearly did not appreciate the name "Betty Hubbard."

Grandaddy said, "What about it, Jimmy? What about Betty Hubbard?"

Jimmy kept shaking his head and waving his hand. He said, "*No know her.*"

I turned to Grandmother and Grandaddy and asked "Who's Betty Hubbard?"

Grandmother said:

Betty Hubbard used to live down the road from us. She visited us a few times and I am sure that she met Jimmy at some point.

Later on, however, someone from the family saw Betty Hubbard. He asked her if she remembered Jimmy. Now most people that meet Jimmy remember him. He usually makes quite an impression on people. But Betty Hubbard said "No." She didn't remember Jimmy. As you can see, this type of social mistake is not acceptable to Jimmy. A lot of mistakes can be forgiven, but apparently failing to remember Jimmy is not one of them.

Jimmy shook his head back and forth again and said, "*No know her.*" He paused for a minute and then his eyes brightened. "*Lite Theron best!*"

CHAPTER TWELVE
TUTDOWN TAUBURN!

Jimmy exclaimed *"Davy Langer!"* He looked at the house guest. He paused. There was anticipation in Jimmy's eyes...an expectation of happy recognition of that name. The hesitant expression on the face of the guest was puzzling to Jimmy. Maybe the guest hadn't heard properly.

"Davy Langer! Blot tick. Tutdown!" Jimmy paused again expectantly, waiting for a response. The guest looked confused and finally said "What?"

This reaction surprised Jimmy. He sighed. His face showed a little frustration. The visitor, conscious that he was the center of attention, shrugged his shoulders. He looked around the room to his hosts for help.

Jimmy walked to his room shaking his head. Some rummaging could be heard, but not too much, because possessions this valuable were kept close at hand. Jimmy emerged triumphantly from his room, holding his tape player in the air. The tape player was emitting the sounds of frantic euphoria. "David Langner!" an announcer yelled. A crowd roared deafeningly in the background, and a few persons close to the microphone were screaming "Yahoo!" in celebration. A broad smile spread across Jimmy's face and his head bobbed up and down confidently as he pointed his index to the confirming tape player. Then the finger wagged reprovingly in the visitor's direction.

In the state of Alabama, there are two traditional college football powerhouses - the Auburn Tigers (also known as the "War Eagle") and the Alabama Crimson Tide (also known as "Roll Tide.") Jimmy loved Auburn (*"Tauburn"*), and like many others, his devotion tended toward fanaticism. He lived, slept and ate Auburn football.

Every year Auburn and Alabama play each other in game that is known as the "Iron Bowl." This game may be the most important event in the state of Alabama each year. The winner of the Iron Bowl claims bragging rights for its team, its school, and its fans over the entire state of Alabama for the next year. There is no season so dismal that a win in the Iron Bowl can not gloriously redeem. Likewise, a loss in Iron Bowl has ruined many impressive seasons, coaches and teams.

In his career at Auburn, David Langner had one shining moment - one great game. But he picked the right moment and he picked the right game. In 1972, Auburn was having a banner season under its legendary coach, Shug Jordan, known simply as "Shug" across the state. Led by its Heisman Trophy quarterback, Pat Sullivan, Auburn was hopeful of victory. In that year's Iron Bowl, however, the legendary Bear Bryant's Crimson Tide were manhandling the War Eagles. Late in the game, Alabama led the game by the score of 16 to 3, and had controlled both sides of the line of scrimmage all day. Auburn fans despaired of defeat - until David Langner came onto the field and fulfilled his destiny.

Alabama lined up to punt the ball to Auburn. An Auburn player, Bill Newton, broke through the Alabama line and blocked the kick. David Langner scooped up the ball and ran it in for an Auburn touchdown. The score was now Alabama 16, Auburn 10. The Auburn fans roared deafeningly.

Alabama got the ball again, and the Auburn defense held. On the next punt, Bill Newton broke through the Alabama ranks a second time, and blocked the kick. Incredibly, David Langner again picked up the ball and scored the winning Auburn touchdown.

Bedlam in the stadium ensued...and it was the jubilation in the Auburn broadcast booth that Jimmy played for the uninformed guest. Auburn won that game 17 to 16, and David Langner instantly entered the pantheon of Auburn's gridiron heroes. His name still commands reverence today on the lips of the Auburn faithful. And none were more faithful than Jimmy. I must have heard David Langner's name at least 1000 times in the last thirty years, and that was from one person - Jimmy. A fellow Auburn fan purchased a tape of that game for Jimmy, and he played it over and over and over again - in his room, on the swing set, and for uninformed guests.

Of course, heroic acts are worthy of imitation, not just remembrance. After that 1972 Iron Bowl, many football sessions in the front yard with Jimmy included a reenactment...a demonstration of this gridiron glory. Normally, Jimmy started by kicking the ball. This fact may seem a little unusual since the act of glory itself was the *blocking* of the kick. The possibility, however, that Jimmy might be hit in the face by a kicked ball - or even worse by the foot kicking the ball - made the decision to kick the ball, rather than to block the ball, quite reasonable to Jimmy.

Now Jimmy kicking the ball was in itself a dicey proposition. Jimmy's kicks involved a windup and follow through with maximum effort. He might kick the ball 30 feet straight up above his head, subsequently looking around and wondering where it went, and almost hitting himself on the head with it in the process. Or he might miss the ball entirely, and end up on the ground with his kicking leg pointing straight up in the air. I have seen Jimmy kick the ball backwards over his head and hit an innocent bystander twenty yards behind him.

Wherever the ball landed, all spectators of the reenactment needed to remember one rule – don't approach the ball when it hit the ground. Reenactment courtesy made this rule important. Self-preservation made this rule vital. Any person approaching the ball for purposes of recovery or retrieval was subject to being undercut or simply steamrolled by Jimmy. A person who did not follow this rule the first time usually remembered it in all future reenactments.

After Jimmy had successfully retrieved the ball, he took off for the touchdown. In Jimmy's world of football, the "goal line" was of dubious direction and uncertain location. He was capable of running toward either end zone...no matter the type or distance of the kick.

As Jimmy approached the "goal line," both arms shot toward the sky - one hand holding the ball and the other hand clenched in celebration. The thunderous roar of the Auburn faithful reverberated in Jimmy's head. When he reached the "end zone," he dipped the ball down between his legs, and then heaved it to the sky. The arms shot skyward again. "Tutdown Tauburn!" he yelled.

But the reenactment was not over. Legs still churning, Jimmy ran to the closest person. He then hurled himself upon the person and straddled his chest for a "victory ride." If the person anticipated this move, then a gratifying time of wild celebration ensued. If the person did not anticipate this move, Jimmy and his fellow "celebrant" collapsed to the ground in a heap. This collapse did not ever seem to diminish *Jimmy's* joy.

One good replay called for another, and the scene was normally reenacted five or ten times in a row. For us, it was a demonstration of heroes and glory. For Jimmy, it was a chance to participate fancifully in a distant world that he idolized.

Jimmy was a diehard Auburn fan. When he was a boy, a number of the uncles had attended Auburn. Jimmy became a "War Eagle," and his devotion to Auburn never waned or wavered.

A few years after the famous "Iron Bowl" comeback, I visited Alabama at Christmas. Auburn was scheduled to play the Texas Longhorns in the Gator Bowl. I told Jimmy that I was going to cheer for Texas since my father had attended school there. Jimmy didn't necessarily appreciate that sentiment.

In the days leading up to the game, Jimmy was careful to demonstrate exactly where our respective teams stood. He held out one hand and made the Texas Longhorns' symbol with it. To make the symbol, a person holds down the middle two fingers of the hand with his thumb, and extends the index finger and the pinkie finger. Holding the hand out, the Texas fan says, "Hook 'em 'Horns!" Jimmy sometimes had problems making this symbol. He couldn't always get his middle fingers in place properly and he would use his free hand to bend them into place under his thumb.

When he finally got his fingers in the right position, Jimmy held up his hand and said *"Tethus Lonhor."* Jimmy then held his other hand open flat above his head and said, "War Eagle!" The "War Eagle" hand swooped down purposefully and smashed into the Longhorns. The Longhorns hand fell limply and lifelessly to Jimmy's side. *"Doe Tauburn! Beat thorry Tethus Lonhor team!"* Jimmy added to make sure his meaning was clear. Jimmy repeated this demonstration numerous times in the days leading up to the game.

The day of the big game arrived. Grandmother and Grandaddy didn't have a television at the "little house." At the time though, Uncle Stephen lived in the "bwick house" at the top of the hill. He and Aunt Loretta had kindly given Jimmy and me permission to watch the game there while they were away. Jimmy and I walked up the hill together with the tension of two close friends who had diametrically opposite loyalties.

Auburn initially fared well that day and Jimmy was conspicuously gleeful. Auburn was winning handily, but then a fumble occurred. Jimmy thought that Texas had recovered the fumble and he jumped up and pitched an absolute fit. By all accounts, he was not a happy man. Not that his actions were disgenuine. My team was the one that was losing. Jimmy acted out exactly what I felt.

After Jimmy calmed down enough to communicate, I begrudgingly explained that Auburn, not Texas, had recovered the fumble. When Jimmy was finally reassured of that fact, he sat down and looked at me sheepishly with an expression that said "Oh! Well, never mind."

To Jimmy's delight, Auburn whipped Texas that day. I was reminded of that Longhorn defeat for many years to come on a regular basis - both in words and by hand demonstration.

A number of years later, Auburn played the school that I attended, the University of North Carolina Tar Heels, in the Peach Bowl. The Tar Heels dominated both sides of the line of scrimmage that day and won handily.

The next time I visited Jimmy, I sidled up to him.

"Hey Jimmy! How about that Peach Bowl?"

Jimmy gave a puzzled expression. *"Peath Bowl?"* he asked apparently drawing a blank.

"Yeah Jimmy. Auburn's bowl game?"

"Bowl dame?" Jimmy seemed stumped.

"The Peach Bowl where Auburn played the North Carolina Tar Heels."

"Wha-at?" Jimmy asked incredulously.

"You remember Jimmy. The Tar Heels. The North...Carolina...Tar...Heels."

"No know him."

"The Tar Heels played Auburn in the Peach Bowl."

"Thorry team." Jimmy was referring to Auburn's opponent.

"Let's see. Who won that game?"

Jimmy lifted his arms and shrugged his shoulders. *"Tan't tell."*

"Didn't the Tar Heels win that game?"

"No know him."

"The North Carolina Tar Heels, Jimmy. They beat Auburn in the Peach Bowl."

"Wait to thee."

"No, Jimmy. The game's already been played. The Tar Heels won."

"Wha-at?"

I persevered. "Man. The Tar Heels sure are a good team."

"Davy" Jimmy started. I waited for him finally to admit the truth. *"Davy, want Tar Heel beat Woll Tide!"*

I sighed. Jimmy knew about that game. He probably knew more about it than I did. But "want Tar Heels to beat Roll Tide" was the closest thing to an acknowledgment that I ever got. Who knows? Maybe sometimes denial is the best policy.

One time, Jimmy and I were walking together alone to the mailbox. There had been some upheaval in Auburn coaching ranks, and Auburn would be hiring a new coach soon.

"Jimmy," I asked as we walked, "who is going to be the new football coach at Auburn?"

Jimmy stopped, pointed his finger at himself, and said *"Me. Me toach Tauburn."* He shook his head affirmatively in a self-assured manner, and then continued walking.

Problem solved.

My initial reaction to Jimmy's response was incredulity. Jimmy was a mentally challenged individual. The idea that he would coach Auburn was unreal. He could no more coach Auburn than, in Jimmy's own words, the "man in the moon."

But the more I thought about it, the more I realized the importance of Jimmy's response. It was important because of what it said about Jimmy. Jimmy did not see himself as inferior. Jimmy's sense of self worth was remarkable. He had faced many struggles in his life, but they didn't crush his self image. Despite his circumstances...despite his limitations, Jimmy's own self esteem was not only intact, it was thriving. The support from Papa and Meme and the affirmation of his family made his personhood whole. Jimmy was exceptional.

CHAPTER THIRTEEN
HEY FWIEND!

Jimmy loved tape players. During his lifetime, he must have listened to hundreds of miles of cassette tape. He had music tapes, family tapes, and audio tapes from Auburn football and basketball games. I can't remember a time when Jimmy did not have at least four or five cassette tape players in his room.

Whether or not all these cassette tape players were in working order was another question. For some reason unbeknownst to me, Jimmy thought I was an electronic repairman. Maybe I actually succeeded in repairing a broken tape player at one point. Shortly after I arrived for a visit, Grandmother would say, "Jimmy has a tape player he wants you to look at."

Later, I dutifully opened the machine up as Jimmy watched expectantly. More often than not, I eventually closed it back up like a surgeon who knew there was nothing whatsoever he could do for the patient. I said, "I'm sorry, Jimmy. I will try to take you shopping for a new tape player while I am here." Come to think of it - maybe Jimmy was shrewd enough to realize that, if he asked me to try to fix one of his broken tape players, my failure would lead to an offer to take him shopping for a new one.

Almost every time that I took Jim shopping, he wanted to look for cassette tape players - cassette tape players and camera film. The fact that he had working cassette tape players back at the house did not make any difference. A person could never have too many tape players.

Jimmy was something of a cassette tape player connoisseur. The irony in Jimmy's cassette tape player shopping was that he always tried to find a new cassette tape player that was exactly the same model as one that he already had. Time after time he found, and I would buy, a new cassette tape player for him that was the same model as his old cassette player.

Eventually, Sharon, who had taken Jimmy shopping many times as well, decided that something needed to change. She told Jimmy that she would buy him a new cassette tape player if Jimmy would give her his old cassette tape player. This trade suited Jimmy, of course, because he was getting a new cassette tape player.

The next time Sharon came to Alabama, she had the obligatory birthday present for Jimmy. When Jimmy opened the present, it was a cassette tape player. Jimmy was thrilled, and gladly complied when Sharon reminded him that she got his old cassette tape player. Thereafter, whenever Sharon came to visit Jimmy, she brought him a "new" cassette tape player. The rest of us realized that these "new" tape players looked very familiar. But I don't think that Jimmy ever caught on to the fact that Sharon had set up her own version of a cassette tape player exchange. After all, a new tape player is a new tape player.

Jimmy loved shopping. Like most forays from home, shopping was a social event - a chance to meet people and interact with them.

Jimmy also loved girls. He had a marvelous way of getting attention - and many times, hugs - from women that were total strangers. If Jimmy was in the check out line at the grocery store and he saw an attractive female nearby, he smiled at her, waved, and said "*Hey fwiend!*"

The girl, who looked unsure of what to make of Jimmy, usually smiled back or said "Hey." Jimmy sidled a little closer to her.

"*What you name?*" Jimmy asked in the friendliest tone.

"Donna."

"*Lite name*" Jimmy said, smiling as invitingly as he could. "*You be my fwiend?*"

The girl glanced around a little self-consciously. Not wanting to be unfriendly, she answered "Yes, I'll be your friend."

Jimmy then leaned over close to the girl. He said *"Weal nithe."* And as he said "Real nice," he reached out his arms as if he was expecting a hug.

The girl once again looked around uncertainly and kind of shrugged. Most times, however, she responded to the anticipated embrace and reached over and hugged Jimmy.

If Jimmy could make the hug last for more than a second, he made eye contact with me from over her shoulder. He smiled a superior smile and if he could, waggled his finger at me from behind her back as if to say "Look at me! I am getting this hug from a pretty girl and you are not."

Later on, in the car or at home, Jimmy would say *"Davy, you thee dirl arm 'round me?"*

Jimmy knew full well that I had seen the hug. He had made sure of that fact. "Yes, Jimmy" I would say. "I saw that girl hug you."

"Weal nithe. She fall in lub me."

Jimmy had some shopping standards though. At the mall, he loved to go to the "Bama Pride/Auburn Fever" store. What I should say is that Jimmy loved to go to one half of the "Bama Pride/Auburn Fever" store. The "Bama Pride/Auburn Fever" store was made for the college sports fanatic. It had team shirts, team shoes, team lamps, team rugs, team underwear, team hats, team pompoms, etc. The list of items with Auburn or Alabama logos imprinted on them seemed endless. Wisely, the store had placed a floor to ceiling partition down the middle, and installed separate entrances so that the opposing persuasions would not have to intermingle. Jimmy loved the Auburn half of the store. We teasingly tried to get him to go to the Alabama side of the store, but he always steadfastly refused.

One time after a visit to the "Bama Pride/Auburn Fever" store, we went to Circuit City to buy a tape player. Duly inspired, Jimmy asked three different women at Circuit City which team they cheered for - Tauburn or Tide. Depending on the response, Jimmy either smiled graciously or turned away in disgust. Jimmy may have loved girls, but he had some standards there too.

Sometimes Jimmy had his own money with which to shop. He often received money from a generous friend, usually one of his brothers.

Jimmy called you into his room and carefully closed the door. He got out his wallet and, with not a little pride, showed you its contents. Jimmy didn't use the phrase "dollar bill." He didn't understand denominations of money. A one dollar bill meant just as much to him as a twenty dollar bill. Whatever bills he had, Jimmy just called them "paper money."

Jimmy did understand that paper money could be used to acquire things. He talked about going shopping and buying something with his paper money. Most often he wanted to buy a tape player or film for his camera. A person could never have enough film. Jimmy could have ten rolls of unused film in his room and he still needed more film. It must have been the artist in him.

When I took Jimmy shopping though, I normally did the buying. I wanted to treat Jimmy to something and he was always willing to oblige me.

I do remember one occasion when Jimmy spent his own money. I took Jimmy shopping and bought him a "birthday" present at one store. Jimmy then determined that he was going to spend his own money for more film. We went to the local Wal-mart. Jimmy got his wallet and we entered the store. We first had to look at the Auburn merchandise in the sports apparel section. Jimmy demonstrated his best football poses as we inspected the merchandise.

Then we went to electronics to look at tape players. Jimmy usually had the tape player in mind that he wanted. He didn't always find it. He was, however, always willing to test drive new models.

The advent of CD technology greatly diminished the variety of cassette tape players offered for sale. This technological progress was the source of some confusion to Jimmy as he perused the electronics display. He picked up a CD player and wondered where the tape went in. Jimmy was accustomed to rectangular slots. Those thin, round slots didn't make sense at all. Jimmy never became a CD man, and we never tried to force the issue.

We finally meandered over to the film and camera section. Jimmy picked out multiple rolls of film and we proceeded to check out. The young lady behind the cash register was friendly and cute. "Welcome to Wal-mart!" she chimed cheerily.

"Hey fwiend!" Jimmy said with his usual charm. The girl forced a smile and slightly nodded her head as she glanced sideways at me.

"You be my fwiend?" Jimmy asked as innocently as he could. A smile and a nod again from behind the register, but no response. But for the width of the checkout counter, Jimmy would have been leaning over for a hug.

The girl rang up the film. "That'll be $10.94" she said.

Jimmy pulled out his wallet and I helped him with his one bill - a twenty. He handed it to his "friend" with a smile. She punched more buttons on the register, showing change of $9.06. She pulled money from the register. "Here you go," she said. Jimmy held out his hand.

Jimmy's friend began to count out his change. "10.95...Eleven...Twelve." When the first dollar bill hit Jimmy's hand, he smiled.

"Thirteen." Jimmy's eyes got a little bigger when the second bill hit his hand.

"Fourteen." Jimmy was now wide-eyed at the third "paper money."

"Fifteen." Jimmy was transfixed. "And Twenty."

When the fifth paper money was placed in his hand, Jimmy just stared in amazement at this unexpected bounty.

"Thank you for shopping at Wal-mart!" the girl said as she placed the bag with the film in Jimmy's empty hand. Jimmy was speechless. He looked at the girl, then at the film bag in one hand, and then at the pile of paper moneys in his other hand. Jimmy then looked back at the girl again.

Finally, with a fervor that showed his gratitude, Jimmy exclaimed *"Tant YOU, fwiend!"*

"Come on, Jimmy," I said tugging his arm. "Let's go." Jimmy happily deposited his change in his pocket and turned to go. As we left, the cashier stared at us with a look that said "I'm not sure what just happened here, but there may be more hope for fulfillment in this job than I initially thought."

Both Wal-mart and America are wonderful places in which a man can pay one paper money and receive back film and FIVE paper moneys in return.

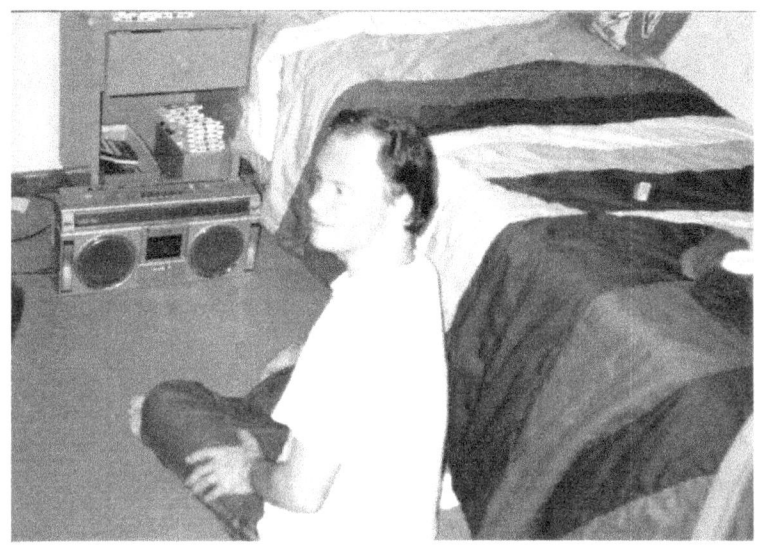

CHAPTER FOURTEEN
MARCH IN WEDDING

Grandmother used to say:

When Tim and Frankie decided to get married, poor Frankie didn't know what she was in for. Maybe it's just as well because she might not have gone through with it if she had known.

Jimmy loves weddings. He loves the excitement and he loves being around so many people. Of course, Jimmy's not the type of person to draw attention from a crowd, or anything like that. (At this point, Grandmother shrugged and gave a wry smile).

Well, at Tim and Frankie's wedding, Tim's brothers and friends wanted to decorate their car and get it just right for the send off. Jimmy was a young teenager then. Tim's friend, Dennis Conway, got the idea that they would not only use shaving cream and attach cans to the car, but also they would hide Jimmy in the back seat.

The wedding and reception went smoothly, and the time came for the bride and groom to depart. Tim and Frankie dashed through the rice shower and rushed to the car. Everyone waved goodbye and, of course, every person there except Tim and Frankie knew that Jimmy was in the back seat of that car.

Tim drove off and turned the corner. In a minute, Frankie felt something hit her leg. She turned to Tim and said, "Tim, stop that."

Tim said, "I didn't do anything."

"Well, I thought I felt something."

A minute or two later, Frankie felt rice hit her leg again. "Tim!" she said. "What are you doing?"

Tim said, "I didn't do anything."

"Well, who else could be throwing rice on my leg?"

At that point, they heard a snicker in the back seat. They turned and, lo and behold, Jimmy sat up in the back seat, laughing and holding a bag of rice.

Well, they couldn't take Jimmy with them on their honeymoon even though I am sure that Jimmy would have been willing to go. Tim turned the car around and drove back to the church. Everyone from the wedding was there waiting for them. Jimmy emerged from the car to the cheers and laughter of the crowd. He was grinning and pumping his fists. After the excitement subsided, Tim and Frankie drove off again. But I noticed that before they left the second time, Tim checked the back seat of his car.

Weddings were special to Jimmy. At a wedding, love and romance fill the air as a man and a woman make a commitment to love each other for life. Jimmy was an emotional person. Love and romance strongly appealed to him. He longed to be a part of a wedding. Jimmy expressed to me many times that he wanted to "march" in a wedding.

At Uncle Stephen and Aunt Loretta's wedding, Jimmy didn't hide in the car. He did, however, vigorously participate in the rice throwing as the bride and groom were leaving the church. His rice throwing was so enthusiastic, he managed to trip poor Aunt Loretta on her way to the car.

Uncle Thomas and Aunt Diane were married in December, 1973 in Tuscaloosa, Alabama. Because of his enthusiasm at Uncle Stephen and Aunt Loretta's wedding, we loaded Jimmy up with bags of rice as we waited for the bride and groom to emerge. It was a cold evening, but everybody lined the sidewalk as the newlyweds dashed to their car.

Jimmy didn't necessarily understand that you were supposed to take the rice out of the bags and gently toss it up in the air. He started pelting Thomas and Diane with whole rice bags, throwing them as hard as he could. After Thomas and Diane scurried by him, trying to shield themselves, Jimmy still had some ammunition left. He jumped out of the line and ran down the sidewalk after them, firing rice bags the whole way. Jimmy didn't see the patch of ice on the sidewalk in front of him. When he hit it, he went sprawling. A collective gasp arose from the wedding party, but there was no need for concern. Jimmy leaped up as if nothing had happened and he continued to chase the poor bride and groom until they got into their car - slinging bags of rice the whole time.

At my own wedding in 1982, I wanted to include my family and close friends in the wedding party. Jimmy was more than an uncle to me. He was my buddy. I asked Jimmy to be a groomsman and to "march" in my wedding. My wife's mother was worried that he might do something disruptive or indecorous. She was not in favor of the idea and let her feelings be known. I knew that Jimmy's participation could be a challenge, but he was a close friend and I wanted to honor him in that way.

Uncle Tim kindly drove Jimmy to Asheville, North Carolina from Alabama for the occasion. Jimmy had been stung near his eye by a bee earlier that week, and he could not see very well. This sting, combined with the emotion of the occasion, led to more than one tear being shed by Jimmy at our rehearsal dinner.

We had more groomsmen than bridesmaids in my wedding party. To solve the processional pairings, we planned to pair Jimmy with another groomsman to "march" down the aisle. His fellow groomsman could serve as a kind of chaperone, and could insure that Jimmy made it to the right spot. At the wedding rehearsal, however, the fact that other groomsmen had a female companion did not sit well with Jimmy. Groomsmen were supposed to "march" with women. Jimmy wanted to "march" with a girl too, and he aired his feelings to the rehearsal audience in no uncertain terms. Jimmy had a way of getting his point across, and he was insistent on this matter. We changed pairings with the gracious consent of others in the wedding party, and Jimmy "marched" with a charming lady, Jane.

Following mountain tradition at my wedding rehearsal, my wife's aunt performed the role of the "stand in" bride. We began the rehearsal. All went well until Jimmy saw a different and older woman walk down the aisle to "marry" me. "*Hey!*" Jimmy protested, using a volume commensurate with the apparent mistake. "Wrong one! WRONG ONE!"

We tried to explain the situation to Jimmy. This rehearsal was practice. It was not the real wedding. Jimmy would have none of it. This event was too important to leave to chance. He was insistent that the right bride participate to insure that no mistakes were made.

At my wedding the next day, Jimmy performed flawlessly. My wife's mother said she noticed that Jimmy not only escorted couples to their seats prior to the wedding, but after he had seated them, he also scooted them as far as they could go into the pews with a wave of his hands to make plenty of room. Jimmy "marched in the wedding" with decorum and did not miss a beat.

Afterwards, my wife's mother, who had been apprehensive throughout, came up to him and hugged him. "You did great!" she exclaimed, with not a little relief.

I don't remember much about our reception. There were so many friends and family that I wanted to see and to speak with. I was hungry, but only could manage to eat the frosting that my wife fingered into my mouth at the cake cutting ceremony.

I do remember the departure. My wife and I walked through a shower of bird seed to a car replete with thorough, but not necessarily tasteful, decoration. As I opened the car door lathered with shaving cream, I carefully inspected the vehicle's contents. Sure enough, occupying the back seat with a wide grin, was Jimmy. He had been placed there by my close friend, Brian Ascher, who had visited Alabama with me and heard Meme's wedding stories about Jimmy. I shooed Jimmy out of the car and he emerged triumphantly to the cheers of the crowd.

From that time on, every time I visited Alabama, Jimmy asked, "*Davy, marsh in wedding?*"

"Yes, Jimmy" I replied. "You marched in my wedding."

"*Lite dat. Lite marsh in wedding.*"

"We are glad you marched in our wedding, Jimmy."

"*Mary Beff's momma hud me?*"

"Yes, Jimmy. Mary Beth's mother hugged you and said you did a good job."

"*Mary Beff's momma lub me?*"

"Yes, Jimmy. Mary Beth's mother loves you."

"*Weal nithe.*" Jimmy said. "*You tell her my lub.*" And Jimmy just smiled.

Cars took on new meaning for many of us at Uncle Daniel and Aunt Carolyn's wedding. The wedding was an evening affair in Clanton, Alabama, which is located approximately an hour and a half from the Wetumpka house. Before the Martin family left for the wedding, there was some discussion of how many cars the family should take. My immediate family was visiting from North Carolina. My father pointed out that we were driving a Ford Econoline van. The van could hold a large number of people. He said there was no need to take a lot of other "unnecessary" vehicles.

We drove to Clanton. The wedding was beautiful, and the reception was joyful. Uncle Daniel and Aunt Carolyn prepared to leave the church. They planned to honeymoon at my family's house in beautiful, mountainous Asheville, North Carolina, while our family visited in Alabama. As Uncle Daniel and Aunt Carolyn were getting into their car, my father stepped in front of the crowd and announced, "Daniel! Don't forget the house keys!" He then tossed the keys to Daniel.

Who knows whether my father had previously planned to deliver the keys to Uncle Daniel in this ceremonious manner, or whether he had a memory jolt at that moment that Daniel needed the house keys? In any event, if those keys could have been suspended in the air between my father and Uncle Daniel, my father could have seen that on the key ring hung not only the house keys, but also the van keys. Regrettably, the keys did not suspend in midair for my father to inspect them. Uncle Daniel caught them and he and Aunt Carolyn happily drove off.

The Martin family socialized after the wedding and helped clean up the reception room. We were some of the last people to leave the church. When we got to our cars, however, my father realized that the keys that he had thrown to Uncle Daniel included the keys to the van. No one had an extra key.

That evening, at approximately 10:00 PM, twenty-two tired, but well-dressed people rode from Clanton, Alabama to Wetumpka, Alabama in two compact sedans. There were eleven people in each car - six people in the back seat and five in the front seat. We were packed like sardines. I was one of the lucky ones because I got to ride in the front seat. I sat in the lap of Aunt Frankie's mother, and was certain that I was going to crush that poor lady to death. She must have weighed all of 98 pounds, but she kept insisting that I was not hurting her in any way.

Uncle Tim says:

I have never suffered from claustrophobia in my life. On the ride home from Daniel's wedding, however, it was suffocating. I came close to a panic attack two or three times. At one point, I almost asked the driver to pull over and let me get out and ride in the trunk!

Fortunately, everyone made it home with no damage other than psychological. Also fortunately for my family, Uncle Daniel and Aunt Carolyn had stopped at a hotel in Alabama for the night. My father was able to call them the next morning and contritely retrieve the van keys.

Jimmy loved weddings. He loved people, and he loved being around people - the more people the better. A major reason for Jimmy's love of crowds was that Jimmy was usually the center of attention. The men talked and teased with him. The youngsters laughed and played games with him. Perhaps most importantly to Jimmy, the women hugged him and fawned all over him. Jimmy liked attention. The bigger the crowd, the more attention Jimmy received. And the more attention he received, the more enthusiastic Jimmy became.

Jimmy's wedding enthusiasm may have reached its peak when the bride threw her garter belt after the wedding ceremony. First, the bride tossed her bouquet. The assembled single ladies exercised polite restraint as they demurely reached to catch it.

Next the single males, including Jimmy, gathered for the garter. The ultimate recipient of the garter belt was almost a foregone conclusion. Most of the eligible men present had played ball with Jimmy. They had been hit enough times that they didn't want to get between Jimmy and the garter belt. Any other young men who had thoughts of garnering the garter learned that a catch was not necessarily final possession in Jimmy's mind. Polite restraint did not describe Jimmy's actions if he did not make the initial catch. After a brief scramble, Jimmy emerged from the throng victoriously waving the garter belt to the cheers of amused onlookers.

Jimmy's most recent family wedding was that of his niece, Christy, Uncle Thomas' daughter. Jimmy was in fine form at the wedding. He talked and teased with a number of the guys. He called me a lot of the usual names. Jimmy reminded me that he had marched at my wedding. He also got more than his share of hugs and kisses from the ladies present.

Immediately before the bride and groom were scheduled to exit the church, Jimmy was carefully hidden in the back seat of their car. Michael and Christy ran through the farewell line, jumped into their car and drove off.

Nobody moved. The crowd stood and waited for their return. We waited and we waited. People began to wonder how far Michael and Christy were going to drive before they realized they had a stowaway on board. Finally, about 10 minutes after departure, their vehicle returned. The car stopped, and to the cheers of the assembled throng, Jimmy emerged from the back seat. Jimmy was grinning from ear to ear as he got out. He raised both arms above his head with his fists clinched in triumph. As the cheering and applause grew, Jimmy pumped his fists up and down in the air and began to dance a little jig. It was a grand event for a man who loved weddings.

Coincidentally, it was a good thing for Michael that Jimmy was in that car. Michael had forgotten his suitcase.

CHAPTER FIFTEEN
NOW YOU LEARN!

Jimmy loved to play games of all types - indoor games or outdoor games. Which game really didn't matter. Jimmy was competitive. He loved games. Croquet was one of his favorite outdoor games.

Most people think of croquet as a game of gentility and sophistication. In croquet, a mallet is used to hit a wooden ball about the size of a softball from one post to another post and back again, through a series of wire wickets. Most people envision croquet being played with social grace on the well-manicured lawn of an English estate. These people never played croquet with Jimmy.

Croquet with Jimmy was played in the front yard of his house. The front yard consisted of sand and Alabama red clay with a few sparsely spaced sprigs of crabgrass and various other weeds. Interspersed amongst these sprigs were rocks and pine cones, as well as numerous walnuts from the black walnut tree which stood in the middle of the yard. "Well-manicured" was rarely a word used to describe this lawn.

Croquet was one game where Jimmy did not want to go first. He usually let a couple of players go out in front of him, especially if they had not played croquet with him before. The first couple of players took their turns, and hit their ball through as many wickets as they could. Jimmy then hit his ball through the first two wickets, which gave him two additional shots. The other players assumed that Jimmy was going to aim for the next wicket, just as they had done.

But croquet has a rule which we called "sending." If, during the course of play, one player's ball hits another player's ball, then that player has the option of "sending" the other player's ball. The opportunity to knock an opponent's ball out of the yard appealed to

Jimmy far more than hitting his ball through wickets. With two extra shots, Jimmy immediately turned and aimed for the nearest player's ball. He tried to hit the other player's ball, and with two shots, he normally succeeded.

After Jimmy's ball hit the ball of another player, Jimmy walked by that other player and said *"Hey fwiend!"* with a silly grin on his face. He went over to his ball and placed it up against the opponent's ball. He put his foot on top of his own ball so that it would not go anywhere, and proceeded to hit his ball as hard as he could. This blow "sent" the other player's ball across the yard, across the driveway, and down the hill. Jimmy then looked at the opponent whose ball had just been sent, said *"He-ey,"* wiggled his fingers as if to say "bye-bye," and smiled a superior smile as the opponent began the long walk down the hill to his ball. Not one to waste shots, Jimmy then tried to hit and send the other opponent's ball as well.

Many times visitors were new to the family, perhaps a visiting boyfriend or girlfriend of a family member. They wanted to ingratiate themselves to the family and to Jimmy in particular. If their ball happened to hit Jimmy's ball during a game, an immediate look of concern spread over Jimmy's face. With an air of grace, the visitor gently tapped Jimmy's ball so that it only rolled a few feet away. With a look of relief, Jimmy said *"Weal nithe"* and everybody smiled at the kind display of sportsmanship.

This good will lasted exactly one turn. On his turn, Jimmy tapped his ball back to the newcomer's ball a few feet away and ...Boom!...the generous soul found himself at the bottom of the hill looking for his ball that Jimmy had just sent.

Eventually, a player whose ball Jimmy had sent down the hill caught up to Jimmy and hit Jimmy's ball. Jimmy would mutter *"Oh no!"* and watch as his own ball was knocked down the hill. Jimmy began the slow walk down the hill to his ball, shaking his head with a look of both disbelief and disgust. Obviously, "*thome* people" (some people) did not understand the difference between entertainment and insult.

When Jimmy got his ball back up the hill, he spent the rest of the game chasing his antagonist's ball. If he caught that player, he marched over to the opponent's ball, wagging his finger. "*Now you learn!*" he said reprovingly. But he did not send the ball down the hill. He turned and aimed for the woods on the other side of the yard, sending that player's ball as deep into the snaky woods as he could. At times, the opponent was lucky to find his ball.

I have played a number of croquet games with Jimmy that were never completed. If you had experience playing croquet with Jimmy, you knew that you needed to put your ball in places where he could not hit it and "send" you. Sometimes, in order to avoid being sent, we hit our own balls down the hill before Jimmy could hit them. Not one to be denied the joy of sending, Jimmy hit his own ball down the hill to chase the other player's balls.

We played croquet games that started in the front yard and went down the hill. The wickets became irrelevant. We chased each other into the backyard, and then around the house.

These games resembled "chase the rabbit," hide and seek, or tag more than croquet. Rules such as taking turns were eventually discarded. These contests ultimately transformed into running polo or yard hockey as we tried to hit each other's balls. The games were rollicking, uproarious affairs, and they probably contained a lot more laughter than you hear on the well-manicured lawns of English estates.

As much as he loved games, it was a challenge for Jimmy to find games at which he could be competitive. Although he tried them, some games like chess or Risk were beyond his mental ability. Jimmy even tried the card game Rook. Most of the uncles loved to play Rook and sometimes they played a big Rook game after supper at family gatherings. Jimmy could follow simple concepts in Rook, like playing the color of the card that was led. He just didn't grasp the strategies involved in playing the right cards or in bidding.

The other problem that Jimmy had in playing Rook was the fact that he couldn't keep a secret. When Jimmy was dealt the highest trump card, the Rook itself, he broke into a big smile and giddily exclaimed *"Hee-ee!"*

Uncle Tim said, "Well, we all know who has the Rook!"

Jimmy immediately tried to contain his delight and said *"No thay word."*

Uncle Thomas, Jimmy's partner, benevolently said "Georrrguh! We don't want to tell anybody when we have the Rook."

"No tell thomebahdy. Thut my mouff."

Everyone at the table laughed. The cat, of course, was out of the bag. Jimmy didn't handle secrets well. He couldn't help himself. If you had something you didn't want known, you didn't tell it to Jimmy.

Jimmy did better with simple games which involved a lot of chance, or games which required repetition. His favorite indoor games included Sorry (*"Thorry"*), checkers (*"Chet"*), Chinese checkers, Dominoes (*"Nomno"*), Rebound (*"Webou"*) and Uno. When we visited Alabama, we regularly played games after the dishes from supper had been washed and the kitchen cleaned.

Grandmother was always willing to play with Jimmy. Grandmother was not a competitive person and did not necessarily enjoy playing simple children's games. She, however, was willing to do it for Jimmy's sake. When we asked Jimmy what game he wanted to play, he said, *"Lite you pit"* [Like you pick].

One of Jimmy's favorite games was Sorry. Sorry used dice and relied almost entirely on chance. Even better, Sorry had the added twist of bumping an opponent's piece and sending it back to start (not unlike croquet). Jimmy did not mind sending an opponent back to start. In fact, he was pretty gleeful about it.

If Jimmy bumped my piece, I said "Jimmy, what are you doing? I thought you were my buddy."

"*Too bad, too thad*" was his sympathetic response.

On the other hand, if some one bumped one of Jimmy's pieces back to start, his reaction was dismal. Jimmy would shake his head in disgust at the gross indignity perpetrated upon him. He had a pained look in his eyes. "*Oh well!*" he eventually said holding his hands in the air with resignation. "*Tan't win dame.*"

Jimmy was an extremely competitive person. He relished winning and he hated losing. Rivalries fueled his competitive instinct. He cheered for Auburn and booed Alabama. When the older uncles attended Sidney Lanier High School in Montgomery, he rooted for Lanier against their crosstown rivals, Lee High School.

In baseball, he loved the Atlanta Braves ("*Lanta Bray*" to Jimmy). Jimmy spent hours listening to Braves baseball on his radio. He loved the team's star, Hammering Hank Aaron, the home run king. Jimmy called him "*Hant Hammuh.*" More than once he told me, "*Davy, Hant Hammuh hit home wun las' night. Lanta Bray win!*"

Some of the other uncles, like Uncle Andy ("*Anfrew*"), cheered for the St. Louis Cardinals ("*Louey*"). Uncle Andy often teased Jimmy about the rivalry - especially if the Cardinals beat the Braves.

"How about that Cardinals team, huh George?"

"*Puh!*" Jimmy exhaled, waving his hand in front of his face. "*Thorry team.*"

"Well, they may be sorry, but they sure beat the Braves last night."

Jimmy's reaction was to engage in a one man pep rally. *"Doe Lanta Bray! Beat Louey! Lanta Bray beat ol' thorry Louey team."* The volume of Jimmy's voice grew louder and louder as he inspired himself with his cheering.*"Yeah for Bray! Boo Louey! Lanta Bray win dame!"* Jimmy's fervor increased as he worked himself toward frenzy.

At this point, Andy knew it was better to back off and not dispute allegiances further.

Jimmy's competitive fervor never seemed to diminish. It extended to all walks of life, not just to his games. But no one really understands what happened with the monkeys at the zoo. We took Jimmy to the Montgomery Zoo a few times. He saw the animals and made comments about their size or features. Nothing unusual happened.

The chimpanzees, however, were different. When Jimmy approached the chimpanzee cage, he became agitated. The feeling was mutual because the chimpanzees in the cage started focusing on Jimmy and chattering.

Jimmy yelled *"Montey! You're juth montey!"* The chimpanzees began hooting and screaming.

Jimmy stuck out his tongue at the monkeys and shouted, *"Doe away montey! Doe away!"* - as if the chimps could somehow leave their cage. The chimpanzees picked up whatever they could find from the floor of the cages, which was usually excrement, and threw it at Jimmy. We backed Jimmy away from the cage. Jimmy was yelling at the chimpanzees the whole time, his face growing redder and the veins in his neck beginning to stick out. The chimps screamed back and fired away at Jimmy. We had to pull Jimmy away from the exhibit forcefully.

On one visit, after we had experienced a Jimmy/chimpanzee encounter and moved on to other exhibits, Jimmy told Sharon that he wanted to go see the monkeys again. Sharon hesitantly took him back to the chimpanzee cage. As they approached the cage, the ruckus started anew. Jimmy pulled a rock from his pocket that he had found and threw it at the chimpanzees. He then dug in his pocket again and located only Kleenex. He promptly threw the Kleenex at the chimpanzees as well. Sharon pulled him away from the cage.

No one could explain the enmity between Jimmy and the "montey." What was Jimmy thinking as he yelled at the chimpanzees? Did he feel that some type of competition existed with the chimpanzees? Jimmy and the chimpanzees both seemed dead serious in their antagonism.

No one really understands what happened with the monkeys at the zoo.

CHAPTER SIXTEEN
HARD UNNERTAN

Jimmy was a sensitive person. He was sensitive to feelings, and he was sensitive to gender. These sensitivities were well refined. Women were beautiful; men were handsome. If a person told Jimmy, "George, you look beautiful today!" Jimmy shook his head in disgust and said, "*No beaufull! Hanthum. Women beaufull; MAN hanthum!*"

Jimmy insisted on his distinctions. That being said, in all my years with Jimmy I never heard him dispute the assertion that he was "hanthum." Demure did not always apply to Jimmy. He just wanted the description to be appropriate.

The gender distinction applied to personal contact as well. Jimmy loved family occasions when his young nieces were present. He hung close to them and garnered as many hugs and kisses as he could. Because of Jimmy's hygienic issues, however, their hugs were not exactly close embraces. Jimmy held out his arms for as close a hug as possible. The girls leaned far forward as if they were launching into a headfirst dive. There might be some actual contact during the hug in the shoulder area, but there would often be a gap of two or three feet at the waist.

The kisses that Jimmy received were often not much better. Jimmy wanted a big "smacky" kiss. Most of the kisses he received, however, were either "air kisses" or a brief pass between the lips and the cheek. One time Sharon, who knew how to please Jimmy to no end, got some lipstick and coated her lips with it. When Jimmy leaned over for a kiss, she planted a large red lip outline on his cheek. Jimmy walked around showing everyone the mark as if to say, "See! When I ask for a kiss, this is what I'm talking about." That imprint required more than one picture.

Men were not supposed to hug or kiss each other. If Jimmy saw a father kiss his son, he said, *"Whaaat? Man tith man on da lip? No unnertan!"* Jimmy shook his head in consternation.

As Jimmy grew older, though, he did get to the point where he would hug or put his arms around another male family member or friend.

Personal space was another challenge for Jimmy. He liked closeness, and the prettier the person, the closer he wanted to be. A year or two after I married Mary Beth, we took Jimmy to the Alabama State Museum of History in Montgomery. Mary Beth says she didn't see much of the museum. Jimmy was behind her every step of the way. Every time she turned around, he was right beside her shoulder. Sometimes he was so close that she couldn't even turn around. Poor Mary Beth started calling Jimmy "the Shadow" on that trip.

At family events, the identity of the person beside whom Jimmy sat was a very important issue. Jimmy wanted a pretty female companion to serve his plate for him and then to sit beside him as he ate. The chosen meal companion was usually a pretty niece such as Sharon, Stephanie, Rachel, Laurie, Janna, or Kay. We guys teased Jimmy about his selectiveness.

"Jimmy, do you want me to help you with your plate and sit by you?"

"*Theron*" was his one word reply.

"But George, I'm your old buddy."

"*Theron.*"

"George, I was hoping to sit and talk to my old buddy Jim."

"*Lub you, Davy.*" Jimmy said trying to let me down softly. "*Need thit by THERON!*"

We, of course, were only teasing. We knew that if the chosen person did not sit by Jimmy, it was not going to be a pleasant day. I took Jimmy to the wedding of my cousin, Angela (Uncle David's daughter) in February, 1993. Jimmy and I were seated by an usher in the church for the wedding. Jimmy looked over and saw Uncle Tim sitting with his daughter, Laurie, a few rows away. Jimmy leaned over to me and said in a loud whisper, *"Want thit by Laurie."*

The wedding had already begun and I didn't want to cause a commotion. "Jimmy," I whispered, "the wedding has already started. You can see Laurie after the wedding."

"Need thit by Laurie."

"Jimmy, I'm sorry but it's too late to sit by Laurie now. Let's watch the wedding."

A few seconds later, I heard sobbing. Jimmy had started crying. *"Laurie!"* he sniffled. *"Need thit by Laurie!"*

He cried through most of Angela's wedding.

After the wedding was over, I grabbed Jimmy and made a beeline for Tim and Laurie. Laurie had the grace to set Jimmy's world right as she fawned over Jimmy.

On the drive back to Wetumpka, it was just Jimmy and me in the car. The male bonding must have gotten to the guy. Jimmy turned to me after a little bit and said, *"Happy thit by you, Davy!"*

I smiled a wry smile and shook my head. What could I say? I had been affirmed.

Jimmy was a loyal person. This loyalty, however, made some choices too hard. As we approached an upcoming family event, we often teasingly asked Jimmy whom he was going to sit beside.

"Jimmy, do you want to sit by Laurie at Thanksgiving?"

"Yeth. Thit by Laurie."

"But what about Kay and Rachel? Don't you want to sit by Kay and Rachel?"

"*Yeth.*"

"Well, you can't sit by them all. Which one are you going to sit beside?"

"*Laurie.*"

"Jimmy, won't that hurt Kay's feelings?"

"*Yeah thit by Kay.*"

"Which one is it, Jimmy? You need to pick one."

"*Too hard!*"

"Jimmy, you are going to have to decide. Which is it?"

"*Wait to thee.*"

"Wait to see" was a response that Jimmy gave often. He was not going to make decision or a commitment before it was time. And no person could cajole, prod, or embarrass him to do so.

The issue of marriage presented another dilemma for Jimmy. This dilemma was a lifelong one. Jimmy really liked girls, and he loved the idea of close, female companionship. If Jimmy saw a beautiful girl, he said, "*Pwetty dirl hyptie me*" (Pretty girl hypnotize me).

He then pointed to his ring finger and say, "*Need wing. Need wedding wing. Need marsh wedding.*" Jimmy started humming the wedding processional tune – "*Dum-DUM-Da-Dum. Dum-DUM-Da-Dum.*" He marched around the room as he sang. Jimmy didn't carry a tune very well, but he had been to enough weddings to know this tune. We all recognized what he was singing.

At the same time, Jimmy realized that marriage presented problems such as where to live, what to live on, and how to maintain a close relationship with another person day in and day out. The issue of a means of support was a big one for Jimmy. Jimmy did not relish the prospect of going to work each day. He sometimes said, "*No me mawy. Too much lotta twouble.*"

Relationship was also a big issue. Jimmy hated hearing about arguments. He especially hated hearing about divorces. Jimmy hated divorce. When he heard about a marital argument or a divorce, he shook his head and said, "*No me mawy. Mite pit wron' one*" (Might pick wrong one).

Deep down, Jimmy must have realized that marriage was not a viable option for him. At some level, there existed a sadness in Jimmy because he was a very relational person who longed for intimacy. Occasionally, Jimmy struggled because of his lot in life.

We tried to reassure Jimmy that we wanted him to be a member of our family. We wanted him to live at the "little house." For the most part, the security of family and home soothed any matrimonial feelings that Jimmy had.

Jimmy's affinity for social interaction did have limits. If he was being goaded to interact with a person against his wishes, he said, "*Too shy.*"

Jimmy loved to hear stories about himself. But he usually couldn't bring himself to tell them. So he asked some one else to do the telling.

He said, "*Davy, tell Meme pway football 'day. Me 'core tutdown.*"

"Jimmy, you can tell her yourself."

"*You doe 'head.*"

"Jimmy, you were there. You know you scored a touchdown. You tell Meme."

"*Tan't. Too shy.*"

Jimmy had his standards. It was obviously inappropriate for him to tell a flattering story about himself. To ask another person to tell the same story, however, was quite acceptable. After all, it was only good public relations.

Jimmy didn't relish all his relationships. At a church that the family attended, a girl named Anna was a member. Anna was also a Down's syndrome person. Anna was as sweet and nice to Jimmy as she could be. She tried to talk to him and relate to him as best she could. Jimmy, however, did not cotton to Anna. She wasn't his style or his taste. Jimmy normally avoided Anna as graciously as he could.

Young children could be bothersome, too. Jimmy did love children. If a little child was cute, Jimmy called her *"kemp kemp"* or sometimes *"kemp kemp lil' kipakee."* If he saw a baby or a toddler, he said, *"Kemp kemp lil' baby"* or *"Kemp kemp lil' dirl."* If the child began to get into Jimmy's things - his pictures, tapes or tape players - however, *"kemp kemp"* wore off pretty quickly. Jimmy would say *"Hey!"* and grab the child's arm looking around for help.

Personally, Jimmy was a man of delicate emotional sensitivity. If something was wrong relationally, Jimmy understood that fact long before myself or others picked up on it. He could walk into a room and immediately tell that tension existed.

Jimmy hated broken relationships. If something was wrong between himself and another person, he worked diligently to try to restore the relationship. Sometimes Jimmy said something that he didn't mean. Other times he said something that he did mean, but he probably shouldn't have said. If another loved one was offended or hurt by Jimmy's words, Jimmy painstakingly sought reconciliation. Jimmy had delicate emotional vulnerability.

When I visited Alabama, I often stayed in the room next to Jimmy's room. At night, Jimmy prayed before he went to sleep. When Jimmy prayed, he prayed out loud. If there was a breach of relationship or a loss of love, either between Jimmy and another person, or between other family members, Jimmy prayed for that relationship. He didn't just pray a few minutes. This prayer wasn't for show. He prayed for hours... and loudly - at times crying and wailing for the subjects of his supplication.

At midnight or later, I lay awake, unable to sleep because of Jimmy's ongoing intense intercession. I got up, went into Jimmy's room and selfishly tried to tone it down. I wanted Jimmy to understand the benefits of silent prayer.

Jimmy turned to me. He had tears in his eyes. He asked, "*Davy, why [one person] leave [another person]?*"

My feeble response was, "I don't know, Jimmy."

"*Don't they lub anymore? Hard unnertan.*"

"It is hard to understand, Jimmy."

Feeling chastised, I returned to my room, and listened as the intercession started anew.

Eventually, after many years, it dawned on me that a compensation had occurred. Jimmy was mentally challenged. His intellectual capacity was severely limited. Jimmy, however, had a highly developed emotional awareness. He was gifted in this area. To the extent Jimmy lacked mental capacity or capability, he abounded in emotional sensitivity. He applied this gift in all the relationships around him - on behalf of the many people for whom he cared.

CHAPTER SEVENTEEN
NO ME FUTH TOMPAIN

Aunt Ann (Uncle David's wife) was in the hospital and it was serious. She had been diagnosed with lung cancer and it was the life threatening kind. If the cancer continued to grow, she would not be with us much longer. We were all praying for her.

Grandmother, Grandaddy and Jimmy were planning to visit Aunt Ann in the hospital. Unfortunately, Grandaddy and Jimmy had been in automobile accident earlier that day. Grandaddy and Jimmy were thankfully not injured in the accident. The vehicles made fairly good impact though, and it had scared Jimmy. Jimmy did not tolerate pain well as it was, and he had bumped his knee. So he had spent most of the day limping around, moaning about his knee, and reliving the trauma of the collision.

That afternoon, Grandmother and Grandaddy walked into Aunt Ann's hospital room to visit her, with Jimmy following behind them - limping. Grandmother was one of the most sympathetic persons on God's earth. She and Grandaddy did everything they could to encourage and love Aunt Ann. Jimmy, on the other hand, groaned, limped around, and even rolled up his pants leg to show Aunt Ann his knee. He aimed to get some sympathy of his own.

Aunt Ann was a very wise person. She fussed over Jimmy and commiserated with him. Ann told him that she was familiar with that particular type of injury. She told Jimmy that the best thing to take for his injury was a cheeseburger and a coke.

On the way home that evening, Grandaddy, Grandmother, and Jimmy stopped to eat supper. Jimmy had a cheeseburger and a coke. Sure enough, his knee began feeling better almost immediately. He made a quick recovery after Ann's diagnosis and treatment.

Thankfully, within a few months, Aunt Ann was better too. She fought recurring cancer courageously for many years. She refused to feel sorry for herself. I never heard Aunt Ann complain about her cancer. Her outlook combined humble acceptance with dogged determination.

A few weeks after Jimmy hurt his knee, Grandaddy, Grandmother and Jimmy were visiting their home church with their close friends, James and Laverne Edge. Laverne Edge had been experiencing trouble with one of her knees and asked for prayer.

Jimmy looked at Mrs. Edge and said, *"You need cheethboogah."*

Poor Mrs. Edge stared at Jimmy with a look that said – "I'm not sure where that last suggestion came from, and I'm not really sure that I want to know."

Jimmy just smiled at her with the look of confident assurance of a man that knew what he was talking about.

Grandmother never held a driver's license in her life. Grandaddy drove her every place they went. When they went out, Grandmother was the "eyes" in the front seat. Jimmy was the "eyes" in the back seat. Thus, when they went out, there was one driver, but three sets of eyes and three mouths.

Jimmy didn't mind expressing himself either. Jimmy had taken a trip with Uncle Thomas when Uncle Thomas was much younger. During the trip, Uncle Thomas committed a minor traffic infraction. Behind Thomas appeared the siren and flashing lights of a motorcycle policeman. Thomas pulled his car off the road and gave the officer his license and registration. The uniform and badge of the officer made quite an impression on Jimmy. Thereafter, anytime Jimmy saw a law enforcement vehicle on the road, he said, *"Uh-oh! Tate out billfol'. Tate out billfol' lite Tombo."*

Grandmother used to say:

Papa and I were driving in the car one day with Jimmy. Papa and I had made an agreement. We had agreed that we were going to help each other watch our tongues. We had resolved not to say anything negative about anyone else. If one of us caught the other one saying something negative about some one else, the person who said something negative would miss the next meal.

Papa and I were driving along when we saw a road construction crew working on the road. Traffic was backed up and it was an aggravation. When we finally reached the place where the crew was working - well, they weren't exactly doing very much. A couple of the men were talking to each other and the rest looked like they were just leaning on their shovels. Papa had worked in construction, and I knew that he hated to see working men just standing around.

Papa said, "Well, would you look at those men just standing there!"

At that point, I just knew that Papa was going to miss the next meal. His tone of voice was not exactly approving. He was frustrated from the traffic jam, and I knew he didn't like what he saw of the construction crew. I waited for his next comment.

But Papa caught himself at that point. He hurriedly added, "And would you look at what a beautiful ditch those men are digging in the middle of the road!" We all laughed. I was relieved that Papa didn't have to miss the next meal, but probably not as relieved as Papa was.

A positive outlook without negativity was something that Grandaddy and Grandmother worked on constantly. They faced significant challenges throughout their lives. In order to survive the rough patches, they trained their minds to focus on cheerful expectations rather than dark imaginations. It was one of the many ways that they practiced their faith.

Grandaddy and Grandmother understood the power of words. They emphasized words of encouragement and of hope. A critical attitude was quickly corrected. More than once, I heard a person express a negative expectation about a situation to Meme. Meme's response was "I'm not believing that is what is going to happen."

Positive thoughts, words of faith, and words of gratitude are a few of the weapons that Papa and Meme used in the battle of the mind. The agreement to miss the next meal if one of them said anything critical showed how serious they were in the fight.

Jimmy was a capable grumbler. We called it "fussing and complaining." Jimmy invariably expressed just how he felt. If he didn't like something, every person around him knew about it, and they usually knew about it in detail - detail which he repeated over and over again.

Grandmother encouraged Jimmy many times not to "fuss and complain." She encouraged Jimmy to have a "happy face," not a sad face. Jimmy tended to focus intensely on a matter. If that matter was a problem or a difficulty, Jimmy just couldn't let it go. The "storm clouds," as we called it, would roll in, and they usually hung around for awhile.

If Jimmy grumbled about a problem, I said, "Jimmy, are you fussing and complaining?"

"*No me futh tompain!*" Jimmy responded.

"Good! We don't like that fussing and complaining."

"*No me doey.*" Jimmy said, shaking his head sullenly.

"Where's that happy face, Jimmy?"

"*Yeah have happy fath.*" Jimmy's face looked dour as if he had just swallowed gasoline.

"I don't see a happy face, Jimmy. Where is it?"

Jimmy turned and grinned at me - except the "grin" was not very convincing. Jimmy's teeth were clenched together with his lips parted in some sort of forced grimace.

"*Thee?*" he said, almost yelling at me.

I knew when it was time to back off, and at least appreciate the effort. "Yes, I see, Jimmy. That is a good happy face, buddy."

"*No me futh tompain.*"

Sometimes the fact that Jimmy had been accused of fussing and complaining was just one more thing to grumble about.

Many times though, Jimmy would take stock of his attitude. An hour or two after a particularly grumpy spell, Jimmy came to me and said, "*Thorry, Davy. Thorry futh tompain.*"

"That's okay, Jimmy. We all have our moments."

"*Me pway Jesus help me. Pway Jesus help me no futh tompain.*"

"That's good, Jimmy. Prayer is important. We all feel sad sometimes."

"*No me feel thad. Feel happy! Feel Jesus in my heart!*"

Jimmy could also express deep gratitude. Sometimes, Grandaddy asked Jimmy to say the blessing over the food at the table.

Jimmy would bow his head and speak slowly and deliberately, "*Tank Lord. ....Duud food. ...Feel duud. ...Amen.*" (Thank the Lord. Good food. Feel good. Amen).

Grandaddy continued to drive until he was in his eighties. When he and Jimmy had the accident, however, Grandmother was not with him. He had dropped Grandmother off at the grocery store. Grandaddy was taking a little side trip to the hardware store with Jimmy in the front seat beside him. When Grandaddy exited the grocery store parking lot, there was an oncoming car. Neither he nor

Jimmy saw the other car. Grandaddy pulled out right in front of the oncoming car and caused the accident. Although Grandaddy and Jimmy were not seriously hurt, the driver of the other car broke her leg. She was an elderly person, and stayed in the hospital for a number of weeks suffering through a slow and painful recovery. Grandaddy felt awful for causing the accident, and for causing the suffering of the other driver.

To compound matters, he did not carry car insurance. The other driver's insurance company had to pay for her medical and hospital bills. Her insurance company sent Grandaddy a letter demanding reimbursement of a huge amount of money. The company threatened to sue him if he did not pay it.

Grandaddy admitted that he was at fault in the accident. But he did not have the means to pay even a small percentage of the money demanded. The threatened action worried him deeply. He and Grandmother had the "little house," but not much else. They lived on Social Security. If the insurance company took their home, it would be a difficult ordeal for them and for Jimmy.

Grandaddy was shaken. He asked me if I could help. I contacted the insurance company on Grandaddy's behalf. I explained his circumstances and ultimately negotiated a settlement for a relatively small sum of money. This settlement greatly relieved my Grandfather. In my opinion, it was the only significant tangible thing I ever did for my grandparents.

Grandaddy did not drive again after that accident, and this decision was probably a wise one. After that, other people - usually family members - provided the transportation needed by Papa and Meme, including weekly trips to the grocery store.

The person who most often drove to Wetumpka and took Meme to the grocery store was Aunt Ann.

CHAPTER EIGHTEEN
INITIATION

In the 1970's, Uncle Tim and Aunt Frankie lived about a mile away from Grandaddy and Grandmother. Jimmy and I walked to their house to visit one day. Uncle Tim had a basketball goal in his back yard, and Jimmy and I went outside to play.

In the course of playing, the basketball net came loose, and needed to be fixed. I went and got Uncle Tim's ladder and put it up against the wooden goal post. I asked Jimmy to hold the ladder as I climbed it to fix the net. What I did not realize was the extent of termite activity in south central Alabama. As I stood on the ladder trying to fix the net, the goal post, which had been riddled with termites, cracked and broke off at the ground. The basketball goal and the ladder began to crash to the ground. As the ladder was falling, I jumped to the ground to avoid injury. Thankfully, except for a couple of bruises, I was not hurt.

I turned to look for Jimmy. He was across the yard. He ran all the way across the yard when the post broke. When he came back, his eyes were big. He said *"Phew! Bastetbaw doal faw down."*

For years after that incident, Jimmy would say *"Davy, bastetbaw doal faw down?"*

"Yes Jimmy, the basketball goal fell down."

"Tim and Fwankie's ole houth?"

"Yes Jimmy. The basketball goal fell down at Tim and Frankie's old house."

"Phew!" Jimmy would shake his head. *"Hard unnertan. Bastetbaw doal faw down."*

I never tried to explain to Jimmy about termites.

Jimmy loved to play sports, and he loved basketball. After they moved into the "little house" in Wetumpka, Grandaddy set up a basketball goal for Jimmy against the outside basement wall of the house. The basement wall was built of concrete and cinder block. A thick concrete ledge two feet high jutted out from ground level. If you dribbled the ball to the basket for a lay up, you had to jump the ledge at the goal to keep from running into it and creaming your shins.

The basketball court itself was hard packed Alabama mud, clay and gravel. It gradually sloped from left to right. A regulation basketball goal is 10 feet above the court. On Jimmy's court, a person could be shooting a 9 foot shot, or an 11 foot shot, depending whether he was shooting from the left side of the court or from the right side.

Jimmy's penchant for repetition was never more evident than on the basketball court. Jimmy would take his basketball down to the basketball court and he would shoot the ball for hours. He didn't have much understanding of technique. For longer shots, he shot an underhand shot from between his legs - a "granny" shot. On shorter shots, Jimmy developed a two-handed shove shot. Jimmy did not need technique. He had repetition. Jimmy stood in the same spot hour after hour, and made shot after shot. Swish....swish...swish...swish!

A lot of times, you could hear Jimmy do a "play by play" of a basketball game while he was shooting. Jimmy had listened to hundreds of Auburn basketball games on the radio. Like thousands of young fans everywhere, he dreamed of playing for his favorite team. "*Tauburn Titers wiff ball....Dame tie......Tauburn shoot......(swish).....Tauburn 'core!...Tauburn win!*" Jimmy raised his hands in the air, and acknowledged the roar of the Auburn crowd around him. It is kind of a shame that the Auburn Athletic Department never knew that if they needed a person to make that crucial shot from one particular spot twelve feet from the basket, Jimmy was their man.

Jimmy was a killer at shooting games. Jimmy loved to play "P-I-G," or "H-O-R-S-E." In P-I-G or H-O-R-S-E, one player shoots. If he makes the shot, then the other players have to make the same shot or they get a letter. When a player gets all the letters of the word, that player loses.

If you played P-I-G or H-O-R-S-E with Jimmy, you better not let Jimmy go first. If Jimmy went first, he simply went to his spot and made the shot. It didn't matter how good a basketball player you were, you had not practiced that one particular shot thousands of times. You might make the shot a few times after Jimmy made it, but eventually you were going to miss. He was not, and you were going to lose.

The strategy to playing Jimmy in P-I-G or H-O-R-S-E was to go first. You moved away from Jimmy's favorite spots, and took the shot elsewhere. And you had better make it. If you missed, Jimmy simply moved back to his spot, and you were dead.

Jimmy loved to win those shooting games. If he beat you in a game of P-I-G he would say *"Davy pib,"* and he would make the pig noise from his throat. If he beat you in H-O-R-S-E, he would say *"Davy horth,"* and he would make the clopping sound with his teeth.

Losses to Jimmy were not easily forgotten because you got a regular reminder. If he beat you in a game of P-I-G, over the next day or so Jimmy came up behind you. He started making the pig noise. *"Davy pib,"* he said. *"Hee-hee!"*

Playing an actual game of basketball with Jimmy was a unique experience. At family gatherings, we often organized friendly games of basketball. If one of our female cousins happened to bring a male "friend" to introduce him to the family, we politely invited him to play basketball with us. We didn't want him to feel left out. Teams were chosen and Jimmy was normally picked on the team opposite from our guest.

Jimmy was a strong defender. In a typical game, he never lacked intensity. On defense, we assigned Jimmy the duty of guarding the newcomer – on this day "Torrey."

"Jimmy" I said as we made defensive assignments. "You guard Torrey, okay?"

"*Yeth.*" Jimmy shook his head vigorously.

"Now don't let him score, Jimmy."

"*Yeah unnertan.*"

As the game began, Jimmy guarded his man. Jimmy gave new meaning to the words "body up." His body was pushed so hard against Torrey that Jimmy was almost leaning on him. Jimmy had raised both arms in the air and gradually lowered them on both sides of his man. Our smothered guest glanced over at us with a look that said, "Can he do this?" We kind of looked away and acted as if it was normal... which, of course, it was - for Jimmy.

As the ball was played, Torrey pushed forward against Jimmy and then stepped back far enough to receive a pass. He faked, made a beautiful crossover dribble to lose Jimmy, and went up for a jump shot. As he was in midair shooting the ball, however, Torrey found himself being moved sideways. Jimmy had recovered enough to get both hands against Torrey's waist and was shoving him as hard as he could. Torrey landed about four feet from the spot from which he took off. His shot likewise missed its mark. It was an "air ball" - about four feet to the right of the goal.

"Isn't that a foul?" Torrey protested. We had to admit that a violation may have occurred, and gave the ball back to Torrey's team.

"Jimmy," I said, "try not to foul Torrey. Just guard him closely." The word "foul" did not mean very much to Jimmy. He had heard the word, but never asked about its meaning. Jimmy nodded his head vigorously as if he understood me and immediately bodied back up to his man.

On the next play, Torrey had a little better idea of what he was facing defensively. When he got the ball, Jimmy was on his back. Torrey was a good athlete and had obviously played some basketball. He dribbled backwards and Jimmy followed. Torrey faked right with his body, then spun left out of Jimmy's enfolding arms, and drove to the basket for a lay up. He drove hard, because Jimmy was charging right behind him in hot pursuit.

As Torrey approached the goal, I just knew that he was going to crash into the concrete ledge under the basket. Just before he got to the basket though, he took off with both feet and shot the ball up and over Stephen, off the backboard, and into the goal. Torrey landed on top of the concrete ledge. His body and arms were flat against the basement wall. By all accounts, it was a pretty move.

Jimmy kept coming, but just before he got to the concrete ledge, he half tumbled and half collapsed to the ground to stop himself. Jimmy rolled onto his back. His legs and his arms stuck up in the air like a dog. Jimmy began fluttering his feet and hands up and down rapidly. It was an upside down "dog paddle" as he giggled. I don't have a clue what Jimmy was doing, except maybe he was expressing the excitement of the occasion. I went over to Jimmy and helped him up off the ground. He turned to Torrey and said *"Lil' Kipakee!"* Jimmy wagged his index finger at him as if to say, "You just wait, fella! I'm going to get you yet!"

After everyone had recovered their composure, Jimmy's team got the ball. Jimmy was challenged on the offensive end of the basketball game. Jimmy was short and he was hard pressed to shoot the ball in games. Jimmy's vertical leap was all of 3 or 4 inches. Since his granny shot started from between his legs, it was easy to block. His "shove" shot that he launched from his chest was easy to block too.

We passed the ball to Jimmy. Jimmy had seen basketball players dribble, but Jimmy never really understood the reason for it. Jimmy just knew that basketball players were supposed to dribble. When Jimmy got the ball, he dribbled once and held the ball. He dribbled again. Then Jimmy picked up the ball, put it on his hip and took off like a running back to his spot to shoot.

When Jimmy got to his spot, he shot the ball. Torrey easily blocked it. "Hey!" Jimmy yelled as if a breach of basketball etiquette had just occurred. Jimmy may not have grasped many rules of basketball, but he was confident that blocking *his* shot was some type of violation. It certainly offended Jimmy.

In a show of sportsmanship, Torrey gave back the ball to Jimmy. Jimmy took the ball with a miffed look on his face. This time Jimmy did not even fool with dribbling. He grabbed the ball, ran to his spot and shot the ball unimpeded. Swish! That shot was automatic. Torrey seemed surprised that Jimmy could make a shot. Jimmy raised his right fist above his head and beamed right at Torrey. Jon was on Torrey's team and had played many games with Jimmy. Jon came over to Torrey and softly said, "Listen! You can let Jimmy shoot, but whatever you do, don't let him shoot from that spot."

Torrey's team inbounded the ball and it was passed to him. Jimmy, whose fervor increased as the game went on, started slapping at the ball. Holding the ball in both hands, Torrey tried to raise it above his head away from Jimmy. Jimmy kept slapping at the ball, hitting his opponent instead a couple of times in the process. When Jimmy realized he couldn't reach the ball, he wrapped his left arm around Torrey's waist and began to pull Torrey's left arm down with his right hand. Realizing his predicament, Torrey shifted the ball to his right hand, and shot with as much force as a man can muster who is being bear hugged at the time. Incredibly, the ball made it to the rim, hit the front of the iron, bounced into the air and dropped through the basket. I looked over at Michael. We were duly impressed. Torrey had an expression on his face that was a combination of relief and vindication.

On the next possession, Jimmy got the ball. He tried to run back to his shooting spot, but Torrey beat him there and blocked his advance. Jimmy was not a man easily outdone. He ran back toward the middle of the court, took the ball back over his head with both hands, and hurled it over Torrey as hard as he could at the basket. The ball missed both the rim and the backboard, and rebounded high off the concrete wall below the kitchen window. It flew back over our heads, bounced to the edge of the yard, and then rolled down the steep bank into the woods. Jimmy was the closest person to the woods and he also was the person who shot the ball. We looked at Jimmy and he looked at us. Jimmy didn't make a move toward the woods though. Instead, he looked around expectantly, as if he were waiting for someone else to retrieve the basketball out of the snaky woods. Finally, Joshua said "I'll get it." He gingerly made the trek down the hill, and through the briars and the brush to get the ball.

After the ball had been retrieved, Torrey's team inbounded the ball. They passed it around until the ball got to Torrey. Jimmy was not happy that Torrey had scored on the last possession and he was determined not to let it happen again. Jimmy got a hand on the basketball and pulled with all his might. Jimmy pulled so hard that his foot slipped and he fell to his knees - but he was still holding the basketball. Jimmy's downward momentum took Torrey down with him. What ensued can only be described as a wrestling match. Jimmy and Torrey both were jerking and tugging at the basketball. Jimmy began grunting and grinding his teeth. The harder he pulled, the harder he grunted and ground. Finally, Torrey jerked free with the basketball and tried to stand up and take a shot. Jimmy was lying on the ground with both arms wrapped around Torrey's calf. As Torrey shot the ball, Jimmy tried to bite his leg. Torrey jerked and the shot missed badly. Say what you will, but shot blocking can't hold a candle to that kind of defense.

We managed to pull Jimmy away. He was red faced and panting for breath. But he was laughing gleefully. It was great fun to him and Torrey had missed the shot. "I think we better take a short break," I said. We did take a break, only to continue playing for the rest of the afternoon.

Like most activities with Jimmy, basketball was fun. His intensity was infectious and his enthusiasm was contagious. Every play was interesting, unusual, and hilarious.

It did not take a newcomer like Torrey long to realize that he was being introduced to a form of basketball that he had never played before. It was an introduction to the world of Jimmy. Even more, it was an introduction to the world of the Martin family. As in most introductions, we tried to put our best foot forward - except in this case we put our best person forward.

It was a form of initiation for a newcomer - the type of eye opening experience that expanded your horizons. And Jimmy was a man who was responsible for expanding numerous horizons.

CHAPTER NINETEEN
BIG TURKEY DAY

For decades, the Martin family has held a family reunion on Thanksgiving Day. Jimmy had problems pronouncing "Thanksgiving" so he called it *"Bid Turtey Day"* (Big Turkey Day). It was not "big" because of the size of the turkey. It was big because of the event - big because all of the family members that gathered together. Thanksgiving was the biggest day of the year in the Martin family. It was a day that we anticipated all year long. If we were leaving Alabama from a visit in the summer, Jimmy would say, *"Thee you Bid Turtey Day."*

At Thanksgiving, we always tried to arrive a few days early - the weekend prior to Thanksgiving if at all possible. The hospitality was too enticing. Grandmother and Grandaddy always encouraged us to come as early as we could and to stay as long as we could. On the day we arrived, we were given the usual warm welcome, and we were treated like royalty. What is more, we had the excitement from anticipation of the reunion event itself.

Preparation for the Thanksgiving celebration, however, was required. Preparation was needed not only for Thanksgiving itself, but also for the numbers of people that would be arriving throughout the week. A day or two after our arrival, we took Grandmother and Jimmy out to buy groceries. Grandmother liked to shop at Winn-Dixie, because that is where Uncle Thomas worked. When we bought groceries, we bought in bulk. On one occasion, we bought three grocery carts full of food totaling $208.71 - a sum that was not insignificant in 1990.

After grocery shopping, we proceeded to a fast food restaurant for takeout - usually Capt'n D's. We picked up lunch so that Grandmother would not have to shop for groceries and cook in the same morning. Grandmother always expressed how good the Capt'n D's tasted. Bless her heart. She cooked so many meals. She felt a profound appreciation for any food that she did not have to prepare.

In the days preceding Thanksgiving, family members started arriving. Each arrival was greeted with joy and with the same hospitable welcome. Grandmother and Grandaddy always wanted as many relatives to come from out of town as were willing - and most were willing. A lot of Thanksgivings we had 18 or 20 people staying in their four bedroom house. People were sleeping on couches, on the floor, and in the basement.

Jimmy was conflicted by these numbers. He loved people, and like Papa and Meme, he seemed to feel that the more, the merrier. Too many people, however, meant that Jimmy had to give his room to some one else and to sleep on the couch in the living room. Jimmy did not like giving up his room, even if it was for some one he dearly loved.

When Jimmy transferred to the couch, it was a major move. He made a number of trips to get everything he needed with him on the couch. He needed his tape player and multiple boxes of tapes. He needed his radio. He needed numerous picture books so he could look through his pictures. He needed his pillow, and some Auburn gear to create the proper atmosphere. It was a major operation.

Before I was married, I stayed in Jimmy's room one Thanksgiving. Jimmy was a regular fixture. He would knock on the door. I would open it and he would say, *"Hey Davy! Chet you"* (Check you). Once in the room though, he obviously was not just checking my status. As he tried to make conversation, he carefully eyed his room to make sure everything was in place and that nothing was disturbed. Satisfied with the situation, he eventually left, only to return a little while later to "check me" again.

One time after Jimmy had "checked" on me, I intentionally moved Jimmy's camera from his bedside table to his desk. Jimmy knocked on the door and I let him in. He looked around the room and his eyes focused on his bedside table. Something was clearly amiss. "*Hey!*" he exclaimed "*Where tamra?*"

"Camera?" I repeated as innocently as I could.

Jimmy kept searching the room. "*HEY!*" he exclaimed as he spied the camera on the desk. He turned and gave me a look that said "I know what you've been up to, fella!"

Jimmy completed a careful surveillance of the rest of his room and turned to go. Jimmy didn't put the camera back on the bedside table. He took it with him back to the couch. His next "check" on me occurred within a couple of minutes.

On the next few Thanksgivings, I noticed that the camera was added to Jimmy's checklist of things he took with him to the couch.

Jimmy shared his room for many years. He didn't get a lot of sleep because his "bed" was in the living room which was the center of activity. Then one Thanksgiving, he got sick. I felt so sorry for him, sitting on his sheet on the couch, glassy-eyed and running a fever. He wanted so badly to participate in the festivities, but he was wiped out. After that episode, Grandaddy did not make him give up his room again and found alternate locations in which guests could sleep.

If Jimmy disliked sharing his room, he hated some of the meal arrangements. The main table was in the kitchen and would seat eight. When enough people arrived, another table was set up in the living room. The adults ate at the kitchen table and the children ate in the living room. Even in his older years, Jimmy was often assigned to eat with the children in the living room. On those occasions, he was NOT a happy camper. Jimmy usually had a (female) person in mind with whom he wanted to eat. Being relegated to eating at children's table only added insult to injury.

Fundamentally, there was a conflict between Jimmy's view of himself and the way others perceived Jimmy. Other people saw in Jimmy a person of childlike behavior and intellect. Jimmy saw himself as an adult that had equal status with other adults. He was one of the brothers and sisters. Jimmy felt that he never should have been told to eat at the "little" table. It was beneath his status.

Jimmy was persistent and he could be shrewd. Many times I noticed that he did not eat much while moping over at the children's table. When some one was through eating at the adult table and vacated their spot, Jimmy got up and took his plate to eat at the "big" table. He joined in the conversation there, while garnering as much sympathy as possible for having to "eat" at the "little" table.

The Thanksgiving reunion required immense work. The reunion on Thanksgiving Day was the main event. Because so many family members came from out of town, family gatherings also occurred both before and after Thanksgiving – large meals at the houses of uncles and aunts; wedding showers for couples that were married that year; and baby showers for new arrivals. For many years, Papa and Meme held a wiener roast on Thanksgiving Eve. Jimmy called it the "*hot daw roach.*" Papa built a huge fire outside of the basement door in the middle of Jimmy's "basketball court." The children loved roasting hot dogs and marshmallows. It was also a simple meal for Meme's sake.

Cooking meals for so many house guests during Thanksgiving week was a daunting task. But Meme loved the occasion. She, with numerous assistants, began full scale cooking for the reunion itself on Thanksgiving Eve. It seemed as if they cooked straight through until Thanksgiving. The aunts who lived in the Alabama area - Loretta, Ann, Frankie, Carolyn and Diane - also planned and prepared numerous delicious dishes.

The men, including Jimmy, helped clean the house and set up tables and chairs. Papa accumulated tables and chairs through the years for the Thanksgiving reunion. He stored them in the shed behind the house. Under Papa's supervision, we raked and tidied the front yard. One time we gathered 10 wheelbarrow loads of walnuts from the tree in the front yard and dumped them down the hill.

On Thanksgiving Day, Uncle David came early with his chain saw. He and Papa picked a tree to cut. Uncle David sawed the tree and cut it into firewood. We carried the wood back to the house. Uncle David was helping Papa and Meme get firewood to burn in the winter for heat.

Then, throngs began arriving. Jimmy got so excited, he could barely contain himself. He laughed, joked, cajoled and conversed with the family members as they arrived. He was always careful to get hugs from the ladies.

We usually had between 50 and 70 people. It was, in Jimmy's words, *"lotsa, lotsa people!"* And the food - the food would feed an army, and it did. Turkey, pot roast, dressing, corn, beans, potatoes, macaroni and cheese, giblet gravy, rolls, Diane's sweet potato casserole, salads - the list went on.

And the desserts! There were so many desserts, we had a separate room just for them - Ann's homemade chocolate pie, Carolyn's pecan pie, Meme's pumpkin pie, Rebecca's deep dish apple pie, and Frankie's cakes (carrot, red velvet, German chocolate…). The choices seemed endless, but that didn't discourage some of us from trying to sample them all.

A lot of the youngsters played football or basketball. They were careful to recruit Jimmy to play. His participation made it twice as fun. The games lasted hours.

Aunt Loretta had her cameras ready and recorded much of the occasion on film. Different family units gathered on the front lawn for picture taking. Finally, the whole crowd posed together. Some years the attendance was so large that the group picture had to be taken in two sections. Jimmy was there with his camera in the middle of it all, his non-camera eye roving around in his head as he slowly counted "*Ooone-twooo-fweee-foe-fiee*" for each picture.

Later in the afternoon, the family all crowded into the living room for a time of fellowship. Uncle Daniel led the singing and the sharing. Grandmother usually held a baby in her lap. She always wanted us to sing one of her favorite songs – *We're A Family That Loves*:

We're a family that loves, loves, loves,
Loves one another.
We're a family that cares, cares, cares,
We're sisters and brothers.
Through sunshine or rain,
We love just the same.
We're a family that loves, loves, loves,
Loves one another.

I watched Grandmother and Grandaddy closely during this time sitting surrounded by their children, grandchildren and great-grandchildren. This time was their favorite part of Thanksgiving. In fact, I think that this time was their favorite part of the year. They had worked all Thanksgiving for this time, but not just all Thanksgiving. The truth is that they had worked all their lives for this time. Grandmother and Grandaddy had a vision for family. Their labors, their sacrifices, their finances, and their time – everything was devoted to building a family together. This vision was the guidepost of their lives.

Grandaddy and Grandmother sat in their chairs soaking in the singing, sharing, and fellowship. As I looked into their faces at each

Thanksgiving, their eyes gleamed with peaceful fulfillment as they watched evidence of the realization of their lifelong vision.

CHAPTER TWENTY
MEME

Everybody expected Grandmother to outlive Grandaddy. It wasn't that this expectation really made a lot of sense. Grandmother was not healthier than Grandaddy, more robust, or more energetic. It simply had to do with how they functioned.

Grandmother organized and ran the household. She knew what needed to be done for the house to operate smoothly. Grandmother did a myriad of tasks on her own. When she couldn't do something alone or needed help, she enlisted another person's aid. Grandaddy was a willing helper. He once said he thought it was shameful for a man to retire and to expect his wife to continue to do all the housework. Grandaddy vacuumed and did laundry. He helped with the dishes. Grandmother's enlistment was so encouraging and so gracious that it made others want to do her bidding. If she wanted Papa to help with something, she directed a sweet winsome smile at Papa and he was her willing servant.

Grandmother was the spokesperson for herself and Grandaddy. In conversation, she took the lead for the two. She told the family stories and the family news. Grandaddy might interject a few lines. If he couldn't remember a name or a fact, he asked for her help. If he thought of a story, more often than not he asked Grandmother to tell the story for him.

Grandmother served Grandaddy hand and foot. She cooked for him, cleaned for him, sewed for him, and generally took care of him. Of course, Grandmother served everybody with whom she had contact. She was the embodiment of mercy and love. We could not imagine Grandaddy functioning without Grandmother. For this reason, we assumed that Grandmother would out live Grandaddy. But it was not to be.

Not only did the big family reunion occur on Thanksgiving, but Grandmother's birthday was on November 25, which was close to Thanksgiving each year. Every Thanksgiving, we spent time eating and fellowshipping with family. We celebrated Grandmother's birthday as well. She received many presents.

On November 25, 1997, Grandmother turned 85. Two days later on Thanksgiving, the whole family celebrated Grandmother's birthday and showered her with presents. Grandmother, however, had presents of her own to give to the family. She gave albums full of family history, important dates, personal notes, and stories to each of her children. The albums were large and lovingly compiled with the help of Uncle Mark, Uncle Tim, and others.

On March 18, 1998, Grandmother got up at four o'clock in the morning. This timing was not unusual. For years, Grandmother arose at 4:00 A.M. She didn't have to get up so early, but she chose to do so. The purpose of arising at 4:00 A.M. was so that she could pray. She prayed for her neighbors, her friends, her nation, and for the world. And she prayed for that which meant so much to her - her family. She prayed for her husband, her children, her grandchildren, and her great-grandchildren. Grandmother had pages and pages of names and places over which she prayed every day. During the twenty years that Grandmother devoted herself to daily morning prayer, no death or catastrophic occurrence befell any child, grandchild or great-grandchild of Meme's.

During her time of prayer on March 18, 1998 though, Grandmother suffered a serious heart attack. She couldn't get out of her chair and struggled to breathe. Although she survived the heart attack, within a few days it was apparent to the family that Grandmother's condition was terminal. Her remaining time on this earth would be brief.

In retrospect, this was a period of grace. Over the next few weeks, the family gathered around Grandmother. They loved on her. It was a response by those persons upon whom she had bestowed care and love for many years. It was a time of fellowship, sharing, singing, and even joy. Grandmother insisted on it. She loved singing, worship and joy because of the love in her heart. It was amazing how a time of sorrow - a time of impending death and loss - could also be a time of joy and laughter.

Grandmother was weak during this time, but she was able to communicate and even tell stories during her better days. She said things like "Jimmy coming to live with us was no mistake."

In early May, 1998, as her condition weakened, one of Grandmother's last requests to the family was "Take care of Jimmy."

By Tuesday, May 12, 1998, Grandmother had simply worn out. She told Uncle Daniel that she wanted to go. She clarified that she wanted to "go home" and pass on to be with the Lord.

The next day, it was obvious that she was failing. Uncle Daniel took Jimmy outside and gently told Jimmy that Meme was dying. At first, Jimmy was very upset. If Meme's passing was a blow to anyone, it was a blow to Jimmy.

After Jimmy settled down a little, he said "Daniel and Laurie (his niece) help me. Keep me (from) running away. They hold on to me." Jimmy gradually regained his composure. He then said he wanted to go into the house and to sing to Meme.

Jimmy went into Meme's room and sang her one verse of his version of "The Old Rugged Cross":

On a hill far away, stood an Old Rugged Cross,
The emblem of suffering and shame.
And I love that old Cross, where the dearest and best,
For a world of lost sinners was slain.
So I'll cherish the Old Rugged Cross.
'Till my trophies at last I lay down.
I will cling to the Old Rugged Cross,
And exchange it someday for a crown.

He then began to sing something that nobody recognized. Although no one could understand the second song, there was not a dry eye in the room. Meme was too weak to respond to Jimmy, but she was alert enough to understand what was happening.

Later that day, Meme passed away peacefully. She died in the arms of her youngest son, Uncle Thomas.

Meme's funeral visitation occurred on May 15, 1998 at Ellison's Funeral Home in Wetumpka. The family gathered before the visitation began. As we gathered, Grandaddy broke down and began to weep like a baby. He and Grandmother had been married for 61 years. We formed a circle, held hands and prayed - led by Uncle Daniel. After we prayed, Grandaddy stopped crying and seemed to do better. He made it through the visitation. Grandmother's funeral visitation book was signed by over three hundred people.

After the visitation, Sharon, myself, and our families took Jimmy to supper at Cracker Barrel. Jimmy was obviously in shock. He said that he needed four people at his house and not three. He needed a "pretty girl" to cook. "Pretty girl" was one of Grandaddy's pet names for Meme. Jimmy also said that Grandaddy (who at the time was 87) needed to marry again.

The next day, Meme was buried at Brookside Memorial Gardens in Millbrook, Alabama. At the time of her death, she left a husband, ten children (including Jimmy), twenty-three grandchildren, and eighteen great-grandchildren.

A few months later, Uncle Thomas took Jimmy and his sister, Rachel, to visit Meme's grave at Brookside Memorial Gardens. Jimmy had not previously seen the grave marker. Because Grandaddy planned to be buried beside Grandmother, Grandaddy's name was already on the grave marker. Seeing Grandaddy's name on the grave marker upset Jimmy.

Thomas gently put his arm around Jimmy and soothed him. Thomas talked to Jimmy about life after death and about heaven. He described how wonderful a new body would be, with no sickness or pain. He told Jimmy how Jimmy would get to see Meme and he would get to be with all his loved ones in heaven.

Uncle Thomas asked "You would like that wouldn't you, George?"

Jimmy paused a moment and then fervently replied *"Not today!"*

Meme's epitaph is a quote from the Bible - I Corinthians 13:8, which says: "Love never fails." It was her favorite Bible verse.

CHAPTER TWENTY-ONE
THE UNCLES

After Grandmother's death, the uncles met to try to decide how to care for Grandaddy and Jimmy. Because of all the things that Grandmother did, it was almost unthinkable that Grandaddy and Jimmy could survive without her. Grandaddy was 87 years old. Although he was still alert mentally, he simply did not have the ability to take care of himself and Jimmy.

The options were for Grandaddy and Jimmy to go live with a family member; for the family to find an assisted living place for Grandaddy and Jimmy; or for the family to find a way to care for them in the "little house."

At one point in the uncles' meeting, someone asked, "How are things going to change for Papa and Jimmy?"

Uncle Tim said, "I'll tell you what's going to change for Papa and Jimmy. Nothing. Nothing is going to change. We are going to take care of them in this house, and they are not going to go anywhere."

And that is what the Uncles did. Uncle Tim, Uncle Thomas, Uncle Stephen, and Uncle Daniel lived in Montgomery, Prattville, Montgomery, and Selma, Alabama respectively. Uncle Tim moved back to Wetumpka to be closer to Grandaddy and Jimmy. Those four uncles committed to provide care for Grandaddy and Jimmy in such a way that a person was present in the house every evening and morning. They oversaw each meal that needed to be prepared.

Uncle Tim, Uncle Thomas, Uncle Stephen, and Uncle Daniel divided the year between them. They made assignments so that one of the four uncles came to care for Papa and Jimmy every night of the year. The uncle who spent the night was in charge of supper that night and breakfast the next morning. He also prepared lunch for Papa and Jimmy, or another family member covered lunch for them.

To coordinate their schedules, Uncle Thomas prepared a color-coded calendar. That calendar was attached to the refrigerator. You saw it on the refrigerator every time you visited the house in Alabama. Each uncle had a different color, and every evening assigned to that uncle was marked in that uncle's color. You could look at that calendar and see which uncle was supposed to be there on a given night. It was an incredible commitment on the part of those uncles, but they did it, and they did it without complaining.

Uncle Stephen says:

Taking care of Papa and Jimmy wasn't always easy. In the first few months after Meme died, Papa was very lonely. He was used to having someone in the bed with him, and he wanted whoever was spending the night to sleep in the bed with him. There were a lot of nights where I didn't get a whole lot of sleep.

And you know that Papa's sleeping schedule could be erratic. He would take naps in the morning or in the afternoon. Sometimes when he woke up, he got confused and didn't know what time it was. He might wake up from a nap in the late afternoon and think it was morning. He would ask if breakfast was ready.

One time Papa woke up in the middle of the night and he thought it was late afternoon. He went and knocked on Jimmy's door. It was after midnight and Jimmy was asleep. Papa kept knocking. Jimmy woke up and came to the door. Papa told Jimmy that it was time for him to take a bath. Now you know how much Jimmy had to hate that - a bath after midnight. But Jimmy obeyed and took his bath. Then he went back to sleep.

The next morning Jimmy was not a happy camper. He came up to me after breakfast and said, "Real hate clean bathe. Real HATE clean bathe after midnight."

Grandaddy could act erratically. One night when I was visiting, I was awakened at three o'clock in the morning by the sound of a vacuum cleaner. I got up and opened the door. The light was on in the kitchen. I peeked around the corner. Grandaddy was in his underwear running the Kenmore vacuum cleaner. My first thought was that it was a very odd time to do some cleaning.

But as I watched a little bit, I noticed that Grandaddy wasn't making smooth strokes for deep cleaning. He was almost jumping around and stabbing at the floor with the wand of the vacuum. It looked like the parry and thrust of a swordsman. I began to wonder if he had gone off the proverbial deep end. I watched him from a distance for a while. I didn't know whether to investigate further, or whether just to tiptoe back to my room and leave the situation alone.

Finally, after watching him dance with the Kenmore a little bit longer, I decided I would inquire. I went into the kitchen and nodded at Grandaddy.

Grandaddy didn't shut off the vacuum. He said "Hey David."

"Hey Grandaddy," I yelled over the noise. "Uh, what are you doing?"

Grandaddy looked at me kind of sheepishly. "It's these water bugs. They come out at night. There are so many of them that I thought I would try to vacuum a few up."

At that point, a bug scurried across the floor. Grandaddy pounced in the bug's direction with the vacuum wand.

Relieved there was at least a somewhat plausible explanation for this behavior, I said "Good night" and retreated to my room.

The daily (and nightly) care of Papa and Jimmy was difficult. The four uncles were the primary caretakers, but sustaining the household was a family effort. Family members who lived farther away like Rachel, Uncle Mark, and Aunt Rebecca came for weeks at a time to relieve the uncles. Uncle Mark even took leave from work for a whole month to give them a break. Family members who lived closer like

Ann, Loretta, Frankie, Diane and Rachel (Stephen's daughter) ran errands, cooked food, and served Papa and Jimmy unselfishly.

Uncle David focused his energy on home repairs and projects.

Rachel (my mother) says:

David was on call for years to help Papa with house or equipment repairs. I have a picture of Papa, aged ninety, tottering on top of his bedroom roof while directing David, who was working on the roof and guarding Papa at the same time. Rebecca and I were concerned that Papa might fall. But David said "Leave him alone. If I was in his shoes, I would want to be up here too."

Until his last months, Papa was still doing some of the mowing on his sizable yard. He was proud of his riding lawn mower, which he treated and used like a tractor. Papa bragged on it, "Why you can even run over little trees and cut them down." And he did!

Papa called David when something went wrong with the mower. David came, got it, and took it to the shop. He replaced the blades, the mower deck, or whatever needed fixing.

Papa offered to pay and David would refuse, saying it wasn't much. Papa never knew how much time and money David invested keeping that mower operational. Papa's enjoyment of it was worth every dime!

I visited Alabama at least twice a year for almost my entire life. When we visited, we tried to give my uncles as much help as we could. Actually, we experienced the best of both worlds on our visits. The uncle who was assigned for the evening usually came over, shared supper, and visited with us. That uncle was able to go home instead of staying the night. Then, we got to spend time with Jimmy and Papa.

The system of care that the uncles arranged worked. It worked because of the sacrifices made by those uncles. It also worked because of the revival of Papa. Everyone was concerned that Papa would be devastated by the loss of Meme. Meme's death was a huge blow to Papa. We wondered whether Papa would engage in life or, as often happens when a person's lifelong soul mate passes away, he might want to pass on as well.

Back at the home in Wetumpka after Meme's funeral, my mother, Rachel, said something to me that I thought was odd at the time. She said, "Papa has decided that he is not going to try to get married again." It struck me as a little unusual that an 87 year old man might be struggling with the question of whether or not to get married. After I mulled over the statement a little while though, I decided that it was a very good sign. It was a sign that Papa was looking to the future. He had decided to live his life positively instead of being overwhelmed by the grief and the loss of his wife of over sixty years.

Papa did continue to live his life. He became much more social and more talkative. Meme wasn't there to carry the conversation. When we visited Alabama after Meme's death, we heard a lot more stories from Papa about his life and his childhood. The uncles who cared for Papa and Jimmy said that they heard many stories about their family or even their own childhood that they had never heard before.

One evening, Grandaddy told me the story of Charlie Hale and Grandaddy's brother, Ray. The story was as much about Grandaddy's heart as it was about Charlie Hale.

Charlie Hale was not a savory character. He was a notorious criminal. Grandaddy's brother, Ray, fell in with him and they started "doing business" together. When Grandaddy was young, Ray and Charlie Hale had an argument. Charlie Hale shot and killed Ray.

Grandaddy said he hated Charlie Hale for years after the shooting. There were times when Grandaddy considered killing Charlie Hale, and if he had a gun and the opportunity, he would have pulled the trigger.

Through the early years of their marriage, Grandmother began to talk with Grandaddy about forgiveness. At first, Grandaddy refused to forgive Charlie Hale. Grandmother kept encouraging him, and reminded him of the forgiveness that Jesus offers to all of us. Eventually, over forty years after the shooting, Grandaddy said that he forgave Charlie Hale and removed the hate from his heart. He experienced a deeper peace in his life when he did.

Another major reason that the uncles' system worked was the change in the relationship between Papa and Jimmy. When Grandmother was alive, she provided care, love and mercy for Jimmy. Grandaddy provided structure and discipline.

Uncle Thomas says:

After Meme died, we all had to pitch in to do the many household chores that Meme used to do. Grandaddy and Jimmy did what they could. But you know how much Jimmy hated work.

One time we were doing the laundry. Jimmy was trying to help fold laundry. He came over to me and he said, "Want old job back."

I asked, "Which old job, George?"

He said, "Old job hold basket."

He was talking about his old job holding the laundry basket for Meme when she hung clothes on the clothesline. Jimmy really missed that Meme!

Meme was sorely missed. After Meme's death, though, Grandaddy and Jimmy began to exhibit a strong tenderness towards each other. They had always loved one another. With Meme gone, they realized their love for each other in a deeper way. Grandaddy and Jimmy began to look after each other appreciatively. They both sensed the need for that level of caring in their situation, and they cared for one another demonstratively.

CHAPTER TWENTY-TWO
OL' BALD HEAD

Uncle Daniel says:

One evening I came over to take care of Papa and Jimmy. I got in a little late and I was extremely tired. But you know that Papa doesn't like to wait on his breakfast. So I got up early the next morning and started to fix it. I stumbled around the kitchen half asleep and put on the coffee. Jimmy liked to have his cup of coffee and he liked it sweet. I looked for the sugar for him, but couldn't find it. I eventually found some and fixed Jimmy's cup. Well, when Jimmy tasted his coffee, he had the funniest look. He kind of screwed up his face. Jimmy kept looking over at me, but he didn't say anything. He also didn't drink any more of his coffee. I couldn't figure it out until I tasted my own coffee. Man, it tasted awful! I had found the salt instead of the sugar and I had put three teaspoons of salt in Jimmy's coffee.

A day or so later, Tim came over to take care of Papa and Jimmy. Jimmy came in and hung around the kitchen, which was a little unusual. But they talked and Jimmy moved around as Tim cooked. When breakfast was ready, Tim called Papa. He served Papa and Jimmy. Then Tim served his own plate and took a big sip of his coffee. Man! Tim almost choked. Jimmy had spiked Tim's coffee with salt! Jimmy chortled and snorted. He was hardly able to contain himself. He thought it was a big joke.

From then on, every time I came over, I had to watch my coffee cup like a hawk. I caught Jimmy trying to spike it with salt a number of times. On other occasions, I didn't see him do it and - boy! - salt in coffee tastes awful. Every time I gagged, Jimmy about rolled in the floor. "Now you learn!" he said.

Finally, Papa had to make Jimmy stop doing it. Otherwise, the joke just wasn't going to end.

Jimmy loved to tease. He had a great sense of humor. The sense of humor arose from a deep love of life. And teasing was a way to maintain relationship. Jimmy rarely teased maliciously. Teasing was a way of establishing or reinforcing connection with a person.

I would walk down the hall of the house and Jimmy would smile and say *"Davy, missy loop."* I looked down at my belt loops and said "No, Jimmy. I got all my loops today."

"Hee-ee!" Jimmy grinned. *"Teathe you."*

Now if anyone was guilty of regularly missing pants' loops with his belt, it was Jimmy. I could usually find one or more missed loops in his pants. I looked at Jimmy's pants, stuck my finger through one of the missed loops and said "George, what is this?"

"No know him" Jimmy replied.

"George, somebody missed a loop."

"No me doey" Jimmy said, as he scrambled to redo his belt, invariably missing other loops in the process.

On the occasion when Jimmy did catch somebody who had "missed a loop," it was a gleeful experience. For the next few days, the guilty party would be regularly reminded of their fashion *faux pas*.

Uncle Thomas says:

When Jimmy played hide and seek, he didn't do a very good job. He would run and try to hide. He could be behind a chair, and his whole back end would be sticking out from behind the chair where anyone could see it. But you know Jimmy, as long as he couldn't see you, you couldn't see him. He could be back behind the chair making a pig noise or even talking to himself, but he was hidden.

Teasing also was a means for Jimmy to attract the attention he craved. Jimmy loved to hide when company arrived, especially if that company was a pretty female. A visitor would be driving down the long gravel drive to Grandaddy and Grandmother's house, and Jimmy would be in the front yard. When he saw the car, he dashed across the front yard in plain view of everyone, and then hid behind a tree. When the visitor got out of the car, she started looking for Jimmy. There might be arms or legs sticking out from the tree and snickers coming from behind it, but Jimmy was hidden.

No one played it better than Aunt Diane when she arrived. "Where is Jimmy?" Diane called.

Grandmother added "I don't know. He was in the front yard a few minutes ago."

Diane asked, "Where is my Sweetie?" Giggles came from behind the tree. "Jimmy? Where are you, Jimmy? Where is my honey?"

After looking a few other places, Diane's search eventually led to the giggling tree. The discovery of Jimmy was accompanied by appropriate exclamations of surprise. Jimmy laughed and, of course, garnered plenty of hugs and kisses. Jimmy said, "*Lite hide. Lite teathe you.*"

Jimmy liked attention and he was accustomed to a lot of it. His sisters, Rachel and Rebecca, got along famously. They also lived three thousand miles apart. When they visited Alabama together, they were inseparable as they made up for the many months apart.

Rachel says:

One time when Meme was sick, Jimmy had a cold. Because of his germs, he was banned from the kitchen and was not allowed to "come on the white floor" of the kitchen. This rule led to a fair amount of complaining, but Jimmy did honor it. Rebecca and I ate our meals in the living room with Jimmy, but I think Jimmy felt a little excluded.

One morning I looked out the window and saw a man walking across the yard. He wore an Auburn jacket and a navy blue ski

mask over his face. He didn't waver in his stride, but came straight into the house and sat down on the couch in the living room.

"Rebecca!" I said loudly. "There is a masked man in the living room."

"Oh my!" Rebecca replied. "There sure is. Who could that be?"

Rebecca and I went into the living room and tried to remove the mask, but the masked man was adamant about keeping it on. You know how shy those masked men are about revealing their true identity.

Anyway, Rebecca and I went back to our breakfast preparation in the kitchen. I told her I thought we would be safe so long as the masked man did not come onto the white floor. Eventually, the masked man just disappeared.

A little bit later, Jimmy came walking out of his room. We asked him about the masked man. Jimmy said he thought it had been Laurie.

Each morning thereafter, the masked man appeared in varying costumes, but he always wore the navy blue mask. My favorite outfit was the Cowboy Masked Man. He wore a wide brimmed cowboy hat on top of the ski mask.

Thereafter, the Masked Man took off his mask. And you know what? It always turned out to be Jimmy. And each time he got great big hugs from me and Rebecca.

Another method of getting attention was the threat to run away. Jimmy would tell Sharon *"Might run 'way."*

Sharon said, "Now Jimmy, you know you can't run away. You know how much we would miss you honey."

"Might run 'way."

"Now Jimmy, you know if you run away, I will have to tie you up with a rope. That way you can't run away."

Jimmy finally said, *"Not weal. Teathe you."* Sharon conspicuously expressed her relief.

Jimmy, of course, had no more idea of running away from Sharon than the "man in the moon." Based on the number of times he explored that option, however, he enjoying hearing the lengths that Sharon was willing to go to keep him.

Actual departure was something that was difficult for Jimmy. Even if a person had visited for weeks, Jimmy always hated to see company leave. Almost invariably, the night before we were scheduled to go home, Jimmy became gloomy. He was not in a very good mood. We called it the "storm clouds," and they were dark, low, and thick. We played games, teased, and tried to encourage and love on Jimmy, but the "weather" rarely changed on the eve of departure.

In my younger days, when I visited Alabama from North Carolina, I rode the bus. Jimmy called it the "freeway bus." The night before I was scheduled to depart, Jimmy would come in my room and say *"Davy, tan't leave. Tie wope fweeway buth."*

Later, when I had my own car, Jimmy would come into the room and say *"Davy, tan't leave. Tate engine out tar. Tar bweak down."*

Jimmy, of course, never made good on these threats. My first car was an old one - a 1968 Volkswagen Beetle. On one visit in my car, the night before I was scheduled to leave, Jimmy came in and said, *"Davy, tate engine out tar. Tar bweak down."*

The next day, I prepared for departure. Departure from Papa and Meme's house occurred just as hospitably as arrival. Meme cooked a large breakfast. She also prepared an ample box lunch to insure that you did not get hungry on the trip home.

After breakfast, I packed the car, and then we gathered in the living room and discussed the visit. Grandmother often exclaimed, "Well, I think that this has been the best visit yet!" We then formed a circle and prayed. Grandaddy prayed for safe travel and then pronounced a blessing. We hugged and said "good bye's." Jimmy sent his best to my family, saying *"Tell you people my lub."*

I headed for the car, but could not leave yet. Jimmy had to take pictures outside. We posed as Jimmy counted 1-2-3-4-5 for one picture and another and another. Then we hugged again.

I got in my car and started the engine. Jimmy came to my car window and told me he wanted to come see "Carolina folk." I told him he was welcome anytime. As I drove off, they all waved. From my rearview mirror as I went down the long driveway, I could see them still waving from beside the house - Grandaddy, Grandmother, and Jimmy.

I set off for North Carolina. My car, however, only made it as far as Tallassee, Alabama approximately twenty miles away from Wetumpka, and then broke down.

I forlornly called back to Grandaddy and Grandmother's house. Grandaddy drove to Tallassee and towed me back to the house in Wetumpka with a rope. Dejectedly, I got out of my car. Jimmy was standing there grinning from ear to ear. *"Yippee!"* he said. He was so gleeful, he almost couldn't contain his delight. My visit was extended by two more days while we fixed my car. At least it was nice to be wanted.

Teasing was simply one of Jim's most effective ways of relating and communicating. A typical exchange with Jimmy went like this:
"Davy, ol' warfwop."
"You're a warfwop, George."
"Davy, lil' culey bird."
"You're a kickapoo."
"Davy, ol' ball head."

"Old bald head? Look up here, buddy. What do you see? There is plenty of hair up here on this head." I lifted my own thick hair for Jimmy to see.

"*No know him.*"

"Buddy, what is this spot right up here?" I pointed to a place on Jim's head where his hair was obviously thinning.

"*Kwit dat*" Jimmy said, waving my hand away from his head.

"I wouldn't be talking about old bald heads if I were you."

"*Davy, big...fat ball head*" Jimmy responded, ignoring any physical evidence.

"You're a bald head, buddy."

"*Davy, big...fat...OL' ball head.*"

"George, you're a nut."

"*No me nut. You big...fat...ol' ball head...culey bird...kickapoo.*"

This exchange usually continued along the same lines for quite a while. Sometimes, I thought that "warfwop" might refer to a "wart hog," but I am not sure that anyone really knows what "warfwop," "culey bird," or "Kickapoo" meant.

What I do know is that there was as much affection expressed in this exchange than if we had said "I love you" to each other over and over and over again.

CHAPTER TWENTY-THREE
BABY SISTER

The care of Grandaddy and Jimmy by the four uncles continued for three and a half years. During this time, the family gatherings continued. They were not the same without Meme. The beauty of her life and our appreciation of the relationships that she had, however, softened the loss which the family felt. The family carried on as Meme would have wanted them to do.

On February 3, 2001, Grandaddy celebrated his 90th birthday. The Uncles and Aunts gathered to celebrate the milestone. Rachel came from Virginia, Mark came from North Carolina, and Rebecca (who was affectionately called "baby sister" by her beloved brother, Uncle Tim) came from Oregon. It was a joyous family time.

Late in the summer of 2001, however, Grandaddy fell ill. Aunt Rebecca came back from Oregon in August to help care for him. She had lost her own husband, Jim, a couple of years before. Rebecca's presence in the home was a welcome relief to the uncles.

Grandaddy's appetite began to diminish. He became weaker and thinner. The family was concerned that it might be cancer.

In late September, Grandaddy was admitted to the hospital in Wetumpka. Initial tests were positive, and the family was hopeful that he would rally. As his bodily fluids were replenished intravenously though, the doctors realized that he had contracted pneumonia. The pneumonia progressed and after a brief illness, he passed away with his family present on September 28, 2001.

During this time, family members were very sorrowful. They grieved at the loss of a father, grandfather, and great-grandfather. Jimmy was distraught. His mood alternated between a state of shock and a state of near hysterics. At times, he laughed uncontrollably, and then he opened his mouth as wide as possible, but did not emit a sound. He looked as if he were engaging in a deep laugh. But it was deep grief instead.

During the time that Sharon was there for Papa's funeral, Jimmy clung to her. He was her constant shadow and demanded her presence during every waking moment.

Papa's funeral was held at Ellison's Funeral Home in Wetumpka. Uncle Daniel officiated. My brother, Michael, was not able to attend, but he asked that something Grandaddy told him years before be read at the funeral:

> WHAT YOU KNOW IS LIKE AN ISLAND IN THE MIDDLE OF THE OCEAN.
> WHAT YOU DON'T KNOW IS THE OCEAN.
> THE BIGGER THE ISLAND GROWS, THE MORE OF THE OCEAN YOU CAN SEE.

Papa was buried beside Meme in Brookside Memorial Gardens. The family gathered at the "little house" in Wetumpka after Papa's funeral for a time of fellowship and consolation. At one point, Jimmy wandered outside and realized that Sharon was not with him. He turned to me and asked, *"Where Theron?"*

I said, "I think that she is inside."

Jimmy said, *"Oh! Theron need me!"* and he scampered back inside to resume his place at her side.

Jimmy's insecurity was understandable. As a very young boy, he had no structure. Now, the two people that had framed his life - that had given him the love, the family, and the security that he needed - were gone.

During this difficult period following Papa's death, Aunt Rebecca stepped forward to stand in the gap. Aunt Rebecca bravely volunteered to spend the next few months living with Jimmy at the home place in Alabama until the family could decide how they would take care of Jimmy in the absence of Grandmother and Grandaddy. Aunt Rebecca was three thousand miles from her home, but she stayed in Alabama to provide the oversight and stability that Jimmy needed. Jimmy's world had been rocked. He did not know where he was going to live or with whom.

But there was another problem. Jimmy was beginning to show noticeable signs of aging and some loss of mental alertness.

Jimmy's attitude wasn't the best either. After Papa's funeral, I teased Jimmy in a way that he didn't appreciate. Jimmy turned to me and pointed to his belt buckle in that same way that Papa had done to him numerous times - as if to say "Things have changed around here now, buddy, and there's a new sheriff in town."

Poor Aunt Rebecca! Aunt Rebecca already knew about the "stock market." During the following weeks, however, she experienced its ups and downs in a profound way because she was administering the structure and discipline that Jimmy really needed. Unfortunately, meeting Jimmy's needs meant that her stock mainly went down.

By stock, I am not referring to anything financial. I am referring to the personal stock market - the stock market of relationships. For years, we had joked about how a person's "stock" would go up or down in Jimmy's eyes depending on numerous factors. One of the major factors was whether a person was present or absent, and if they were absent, how long the absence had been and how far away they were. If a person that Jimmy liked had been absent a long time, that person's "stock" could reach a very high or elevated status.

In the case of Rachel, Aunt Rebecca, and Sharon, the stock could even reach "Goddess" status. If Aunt Rebecca, living in Oregon, had not visited for a number of months, Jimmy talked on and on about how wonderful she was, how much he missed her, and how much he wanted to see her. Her stock soared.

Conversely, if that same person visited Alabama, the "Goddess" status dissipated in about twenty-four hours. Thereafter, the longer that person stayed, the lower the stock fell. It continued to plummet until that person prepared to leave.

The simple truth was that at times Jimmy could be a very difficult person to live with. His penchant for repetition alone could drive you to distraction. For Jimmy, a fact was just as interesting the hundredth time as it was the first time. He simply did not understand why other people did not have the same fascination with the same statement upon hearing it the hundredth time as the first time. His personal habits and noises could be also annoying, and his hygiene could be disgusting. Finally, Jimmy was stubborn and persistent. If a person was not careful, the patience would wear thin.

When we used to joke about the stock market or about Goddess status, the one person who seemed to appreciate those comments the most was Meme. When we talked about the stock market, Meme shook her head knowingly. Only she knew day after day, week after week, and year after year, what it meant to be Jimmy's primary care giver. She had sacrificed many years of her life for Jimmy.

Now, it was Aunt Rebecca's turn. By the time of Papa's funeral, her stock was already plummeting. She lost her father, and on top of that had to try to deal with Jimmy who was shaken and uncertain. When we returned for the family reunion at Thanksgiving two months later, Aunt Rebecca's stock had reached the depth of depression. Aunt Rebecca was simply not a highly appreciated person. Jimmy resented being told what to do by his sister and he let everyone know it. It was a difficult time.

Jimmy's disposition immediately before Thanksgiving was not cheery. Sharon called to tell us when she would arrive. A huge mistake was made, however, because we did not put Jimmy on the phone to talk with Sharon when she called. Just when we thought Jimmy's mood could not go lower, it did. But Aunt Rebecca's sacrifice did inspire a poem of appreciation. The poem read as follows:

THANK YOU, BABY SISTER

'Twas the day before Big Turkey,
and all through the house,
our faces were crestfallen.
We were as low as a louse.

For Sharon had called,
but she had not conversed.
The storm clouds had settled.
Matters could only get worse.

When out on the driveway,
there arose such a sight,
I leapt from my doldrums,
hoping for a van colored white.

From the ledge of my window,
I peered out the side.
I quickly reviewed my list of
the places I could hide.

"On Andrew, on Mary"
her voice was a-jingling.
It rang in the carport,
and set my ear wax a-tingling.

She stepped down from her sleigh.
She stood five foot two.
Her nose was not cherry red,
but her eyes sparkled blue.

A shout rang from the kitchen.
Jubilation suddenly thrived.
The household was rejoicing for
The Great Sharon Had Arrived!

Sharon indeed had arrived, and for a few days of fellowship and remembrance, the Martin family embraced each other and embraced Jimmy. The family though, did not know what to do to care for Jimmy. Jimmy had never been formally adopted. He came to the Martin family in an informal foster care situation, and he simply never left.

Uncle Tim arranged for a guardianship proceeding for Jimmy. The purpose of the proceeding was to give Jimmy a legal representative. Tim was appointed as Jim's guardian with other uncles listed as alternate guardians. Tim took Jimmy to a Magistrate to obtain the guardianship. As Jimmy often did, he wanted to socialize with the Magistrate. If Jimmy was in a public setting and wanted to say something, he said, *"Lite thay word."*

"Like say a word" applied to the guardianship hearing. Jimmy told the Magistrate about his family, about Papa and Meme and his brothers and sisters. He told the Magistrate more than the Magistrate wanted to hear, but Jimmy did consent to the guardianship, and the Order was entered.

The experience with Aunt Rebecca showed though, that it would be very difficult for any of the uncles or aunts to care for Jimmy. It was not unusual for a Downs syndrome person of Jimmy's age to suffer from dementia, and Jimmy was showing some initial stages of it. But no one wanted to see Jimmy placed in an institution.

Uncle Daniel sacrificially offered for Jimmy to come live with him. That arrangement seemed to be the best option available and the family was preparing to do it until an unexpected alternative presented itself. The alternative was at first a surprise in that it would even be considered. But ultimately it was a blessing due to the positive impact that it had.

CHAPTER TWENTY-FOUR
DOD KNOWS

Uncle Stephen says:
We were all in kind of a conundrum about Jimmy after Papa died. Daniel had offered to take him, but we knew it would be very difficult. Whatever we did was going to be difficult for Jimmy too.

I heard about Rainbow from my church. I was skeptical about it. Jimmy had lived with family all his life. The last thing we wanted was for Jimmy to be placed in a group home or some type of long term care center. We really didn't think Rainbow was an option. But I figured it wouldn't do any harm to check it out. So a few of us got in the car to go see Rainbow. In fact, I think that Jimmy went with us on that first visit.

You know when we got there and saw Rainbow - saw how they operated and the services they provided - it changed our minds. They have a first class operation up there. But the most important thing was that they cared for the residents there. We decided Rainbow might be just what Jimmy needed.

Of course, when we came back and told the other family members about Rainbow, they were skeptical too. But as each person went up to check Rainbow out, the same thing happened. Seeing Rainbow made them realize that it could be really good for Jimmy. So we decided to give it a try.

When we met with the Rainbow staff about Jimmy, they told us the transition could be difficult. Each new resident has a 90 day probationary period to see if Rainbow is right for them. We were a little concerned about Jimmy. You know that he doesn't like change. He wanted his room at the "little house" in Wetumpka. But he made it through the probationary period and eventually Rainbow became his new home.

Rainbow Omega is a private care community for special needs persons located in Eastaboga, Alabama. Eastaboga is near Anniston, about an hour and half drive north of Wetumpka. I first saw Rainbow on the way to a Thanksgiving reunion. We arranged to pick up Jimmy on Thanksgiving Eve to take him with us to Uncle Thomas' house where we were staying.

When I logged onto the Rainbow website to confirm driving directions to Rainbow, the site had a group picture of the residents. All of the residents were smiling and looking at the camera - all the residents, that is, but one. One resident had his back turned to the camera and had his arms in the air, gesticulating about something. I said, "Mary Beth, that looks like Jimmy! But the back of his jacket says 'Bears.'"

I thought for a minute. Jimmy had a "Bears" jacket that he really liked. The colors of the jacket were close to Auburn colors and he probably thought it was an Auburn jacket. Jimmy was the lone nonconforming resident in the Rainbow group picture.

Rainbow Omega is located just outside of Eastaboga on a large campus. On the main road, there is small store that sells nursery plants and landscaping bushes raised by Rainbow residents. As you enter the Rainbow complex, you see nursery greenhouses on the left. The administrative office and welcome center for visitors is located at the bottom of the hill. Behind this office is a large metal building the size of a large gymnasium - the vocational building. In the left half of this building is the kitchen and dining hall to feed residents. In the right half of this building is a large work area furnished with many work stations.

One of the major goals of the Rainbow program is to enhance the self esteem of its participants through vocation and productivity. Rainbow residents can work raising plants in the field and greenhouses; or they can work indoors at the work stations on tasks such as sorting and packaging items. The residents are paid for their production. Every couple of weeks, a bank in Eastaboga closes early, and allows the Rainbow residents to deposit or to cash their checks.

Rainbow takes its residents on frequent field trips. They go shopping so residents can spend the money that they earn. There are recreational outings for bowling, movies, or games. These trips reward the good work and good behavior of the residents.

Uncle Stephen says:

The work program at Rainbow is a great program. It is designed to help the self esteem of the residents and to give them something to do with their time. The residents can learn how to do a lot of different tasks. Well, you know how much Jimmy likes work.

A few months after Jimmy had been at Rainbow, I went up to see him. I noticed that he wasn't working when I got there. I asked him about it, and he told me that he had been "fired" from his job at Rainbow. You know, I don't know what happened, but only Jimmy could have gotten himself fired by Rainbow.

Multiple residence halls or "group homes" at Rainbow are located higher up the hill behind the vocational building. Each home has eight rooms for residents with connecting bathrooms. The home also has a recreational living area/den and a kitchen. Every residence has a "house manager" that provides care for the residents. This personal care of the residents is a marvelous benefit of the Rainbow program. One of Jimmy's favorite managers was named Wayne.

Wayne says:

One time I took Jimmy out to eat. Jimmy wanted a hamburger and french fries so we went to a local fast food restaurant. I got Jimmy his meal and I ordered chicken nuggets. We sat down and

Jimmy gobbled down his meal. When Jimmy was finished, he began eyeing my meal as I ate.

Jimmy pointed to my chicken nuggets and asked "What's that?"

I replied "That's chicken."

Jimmy looked up at me and said *"Yeah lite shi-ken."*

I paused for a minute, and then I offered him the rest of my nuggets which he gobbled down as well.

When I went into Jimmy's group home to pick him up, I told the house manager that I was there to get Jimmy. Jimmy was standing around the corner and he heard my voice. He said *"Davy!"* The sheer joy in his voice alone made the trip worthwhile. Jimmy showed me his room at Rainbow, but he was obviously ready to leave for Thanksgiving. He had an attitude that said, "Let's get out of here." I noticed though, that his other house residents said "Goodbye!", "We'll miss you!" and "Come back soon, Jimmy!" as he left.

When we got into the car, Jimmy was very excited. I asked Jimmy if he was hungry. He said he was.

"Jimmy," I asked "would you like to go out to eat?"

"You doe 'head."

"What would you like to eat?"

"Hamboodah, fren fry, tote, ifream."

We took Jimmy to a local fast food place and got him a hamburger, french fries, Coke and an ice cream cone. He ate his meal with relish.

The trip after the meal to Uncle Thomas' house in Prattville was high energy. We had to fight rush hour traffic on Thanksgiving Eve in Birmingham which alone was nerve wracking.

To assist me in my driving, I had a loud and giddy Jimmy sitting beside me whose already excited state was enhanced by caffeine and sugar. He was talking a mile a minute. There were multiple *"culey bird's,*" "*kickapoo's*" and "*warfwop's.*" He poked me with his finger to tickle me, and grabbed the loops of my belt and kept telling me that I had missed them. I kept telling myself that IF we made it to Prattville in one piece, it would be one of the most memorable drives of my life.

That first time I picked up Jimmy from Rainbow, he was ready to leave. He wanted to see his family and go back to familiar places. After we were in the car a few minutes, Jimmy said, "*Davy, need ol' woom. Need ol' woom at lil' houth.*"

I said "Jimmy, what about Rainbow?"

"*No know him!*" Jimmy said.

After a year though, Rainbow became "home" to Jimmy. Jimmy adjusted to the setting and to the structured lifestyle that Rainbow provided. Later on, when Jimmy said, "*Need doe home,*" he was referring to Rainbow.

Uncle Daniel says:

I want to tell you how well Jimmy adjusted to Rainbow. All of my siblings have Bible names - Rachel, Mark, Stephen, David, Rebecca, Tim, Daniel, Andrew, Thomas and even James - for Jimmy. We've all got Bible names. As Jimmy's dementia was setting in, I would start asking Jimmy to name his brothers and sisters which is a pretty good chore. And he can never name all of us, but all of a sudden there is a new one in the mix - Wayne! And Wayne is not a Bible name. But he's our brother now! Wayne is a house manager that Jimmy just fell in love with. Wayne's our brother now. Now it's *nine* boys and two girls.

We can never say enough about what Rainbow Omega has meant to us.

Besides Wayne, Jimmy also became close to his "row leader" in the vocational center. Her name was Jan. Jan and Wayne were probably Jimmy's two favorite people at Rainbow.

When Jimmy was at Rainbow Omega, the staff of Rainbow Omega did a great job of arranging activities for the Rainbow Omega residents. Rainbow Omega had a number of notable supporters from the athletic world. One of the main contributors was Gene Stallings, former head football coach for the University of Alabama. Coach Stallings devoted a lot of time to the Rainbow Omega organization, not just in fundraising, but interacting with the Rainbow Omega residents. In Jimmy's mind, Coach Stallings was fine, but he had coached the "wrong team" – Auburn's archrival, Alabama.

Through Rainbow, Jimmy was also able to meet Pat Dye, former head football coach at Auburn. This meeting was definitely a thrill for Jimmy. He felt a common bond with Coach Dye, and was duly impressed.

The transition to Rainbow was a difficult one for Jimmy. During a time of grief, he experienced a complete change of location, habitat, and culture. When he first arrived at Rainbow, he had no friends. His caretakers were strangers. What sustained Jimmy during this time?

Uncle Daniel says:

Jimmy has a lot of sayings - a lot of things that are just unique to him. When anything happens that is beyond his understanding - that he can't handle or he can't deal with - or when he doesn't know what to do, he has a two word saying that just totally defuses all the pressure and the stress. Jimmy just says *"Dod knows. Dod knows."*

"God knows." You know what? I've used that a lot myself. I'm not any different from him. I hit the wall sometimes and I don't know how to cope with things or how to deal with things. I've learned to just back off and say, "God knows. God knows."

You know what? God does know!

CHAPTER TWENTY-FIVE
HARD AS BWICK

Jimmy was a man of determination. Like all of us, he experienced failure in some of his endeavors. When he failed though, it was rarely due to a lack of resolve or effort. Jimmy had strong force of will.

Uncle Tim says:

When he was young, Jimmy did respond to Papa's discipline with the belt. Strangely enough, Jimmy would never cry when Papa spanked him. The rest of us children would cry immediately when given a whipping. Our crying seemed to assure Papa that the discipline was effective and being administered properly. But not so with Jimmy. He simply would not cry when Papa spanked him! This fact frustrated Papa considerably.

In Jimmy's later years, I asked Jimmy why he wouldn't cry when Papa spanked him. I asked him this question just so I could hear his response. Jimmy would laugh heartily and say, "*My tail hard as bwick!*"

Rachel says:

With Papa and Jimmy, it was sometimes a case of the irresistible force meeting the immovable object. Of course, neither of them had much use for negotiation! Jimmy respected Papa and he obeyed him. But I think that they learned a lot from each other. Meme was often the buffer between them.

One area of contention for Jimmy in later years was the church that Papa and Meme attended. In prior years, the family had attended larger churches. As Grandaddy and Grandmother grew older though, on Sunday mornings they started attending "church" at the home of their next door neighbors, James and Laverne Edge.

The meeting began by watching the sermon of a reputable television preacher. Then there was singing accompanied by "Sister" Edge on the organ. Next, either Papa or "Brother" Edge shared a lesson, followed by prayer and communion. The meeting was regularly attended by five people - Mr. and Mrs. Edge, Papa and Meme, and Jimmy. This arrangement was convenient and comfortable for Papa and Meme. Transportation became increasingly difficult as they aged, and the Edges were close friends. Four out of the five participants were very satisfied by this arrangement.

The fifth participant, however, was not at all pleased with this arrangement. Jimmy didn't necessarily object to the form of worship, and he didn't dislike Brother or Sister Edge. They welcomed him and tried to involve him as much as possible. Jimmy objected to the lack of a crowd. Jimmy had a good understanding of the word "fellowship," and he liked the interactive fellowship offered by the larger congregations that the Martin family had attended in years past.

Jimmy let his feelings be known to anyone he could. When we visited, Jimmy would say, *"No lite lil' church. Lite ole church best."* Jimmy expressed this sentiment often enough that Grandaddy told him to quit mentioning it. The family was going to attend church at the Edge's - case closed. Grandaddy didn't want to hear another word about it.

Jimmy still found a way to express his feelings. One hymn that Jimmy remembered from one of the larger churches he had attended was the invitation hymn *"Why Not Tonight?"* It was a hymn sung at the end of the service during an altar call. For Jimmy, it symbolized a different church. After Grandaddy squelched Jimmy's open dissent, Jimmy would come up behind you and start softly singing or humming *"Why Not Tonight?"* He did it over and over and over again.

On one visit, Sharon said if she heard the strains of *"Why Not Tonight?"* one more time, she was going to scream. Jimmy honored Grandaddy's command, but it did not prevent him from issuing a regular reminder of where he stood.

Jimmy's determination was evident in many other areas. On one Alabama visit, I went to the golf driving range near Wetumpka. As usual, Jimmy wanted to go with me. To a person who has not played the game of golf, hitting a golf ball appears to be an effortless and easy task. A person who has never hit a golf ball though, often misses the ball completely on his first swing. It is amazing how hard it is to hit a ball that is lying still and motionless.

I was dubious about Jimmy's chances at the driving range. Jimmy had never hit a golf ball and his eyesight was not the best. To compound his problems, Jimmy had to hit the golf ball backwards. Jimmy was right-handed, but I had left-handed clubs. Despite these obstacles, Jimmy wasn't going to sit and watch me hit balls. He wanted to hit golf balls regardless of the challenge.

Jimmy's driving range experience was difficult. He sometimes swung 3 or 4 times just to make contact with the ball. He swung, and he swung, and he swung - veritably flailing at the ball. Every miss of the ball, however, only made him more determined to hit it the next time.

When Jimmy did make contact, the ball had an erratic flight and an uncertain destiny. As a result, Jimmy managed to keep other golfers at the driving range on their toes. After Jimmy had unleashed a few scattering shots, I noticed the glances from nearby patrons change from curiosity to nervousness. Only when the ball bucket was empty though, did Jimmy cease his determined efforts.

In the midst of the red clay and scrub pine about a quarter of a mile from Papa and Meme's house in Wetumpka was "the canyon."

The canyon had eroded through years of rain washing over sparsely covered ground. Open and accessible on the lower northern end, it was 30 feet wide in the middle, and had walls that ranged from 20 to 30 feet high.

For us children, the canyon was a place of wonderment and awe. We loved exploring its topographical and geologic features. The canyon had ridges that rose like buttresses from the floor of the canyon up to the rim of the canyon. We played in the canyon and climbed all over it.

Jimmy generally went with us to the canyon. For Jimmy though, the canyon did not hold the same delights. A person had to go through woods and underbrush to get into the canyon. Sometimes Jimmy just sat out near the road while we played in the canyon and waited for us. Usually though, he crept through the bushy growth to get into the canyon. He stepped high and kept a watchful eye for the movement of any creatures slithering in the brush. Jimmy wanted another person in front of him as he made his way into the canyon, and he stayed not more than a foot or two behind that person the whole way.

Once he was safely in the canyon, Jimmy did not do any climbing. Jimmy had a healthy fear of heights. I don't remember seeing Jimmy climb a ladder. He wanted his two feet firmly on the ground. Even stairs were ascended slowly and carefully.

One time Jimmy visited the canyon with my brothers and me. Once inside the canyon, we began playing and climbing. Eventually, all of us had climbed up a ridge to the top of the canyon and were standing on the rim. All of us, that is - except Jimmy. He was still down on the canyon floor looking up at us. We began urging Jimmy to come up and join us. Jimmy obviously did not like that idea. We egged him on - alternately encouraging him and ragging him. We were "up here," and Jimmy was still "down there."

Maybe Jimmy had an adventurous spirit that day. Maybe he didn't like the fact that even "little people" like my younger brothers, Michael and Arthur, had done it, but he had not. Maybe it was peer pressure. Anyway, in the midst of all that group encouragement, Jimmy made a decision to try to climb the canyon wall.

To the sound of our cheers, Jimmy began to climb the canyon ridge. He slowly went up the lower slope, slipping back a couple of times in the soft sand at the base. Each time he slipped, he paused a little bit, and then tried again. The grinding of his teeth against one another could be heard all the way up top. Once Jimmy got a foothold on the slope, he plastered himself against the wall like ground cover. The red clay stained his pants, arms, and t-shirt.

As we rooted for him, Jimmy inched up the slope until he got to the lower ridge line. Using his limberness, he stretched up a foot and pulled his body around straddling the ridge with his legs like a saddle. Jimmy was red faced and stopped for a couple of moments. He was breathing heavily. We wondered if he would continue.

Still astride the ridge, Jimmy pulled himself up the ridge line lifting his body with his hands in front. Leaning forward, Jimmy kept his torso as close to the ridge as he could. He reached the point where the ridge was too steep for his "saddle" technique. Jimmy slowly got up on all fours and gingerly crawled up the slope.

Jimmy finally reached a ledge below the canyon rim. We were almost beside ourselves with excitement. The last few feet though, were the toughest. Jimmy was eight feet from the top. The canyon wall at that point was almost vertical and there were not any secure footholds. Jimmy was stranded in "no man's land." He stopped and crouched on the ledge. He didn't want to risk the final lunge, but he didn't want to go back down either. He was a few feet away from us, but must have felt very alone.

We reached our hands down and told Jimmy to grab hold. It was uncertain whether he trusted anything at that point. He stretched out his arms, but could barely touch our hands.

But the next moment he made a commitment. Jimmy stepped onto a small hole in the canyon wall and lunged for my arm. As he strained upward, his lips parted and revealed teeth that were clenched in determination. Jimmy grabbed my hand. I pulled and he scrambled - rolling his body up over the top.

Jimmy lay on the ground for a minute, breathing heavily. He was dripping with sweat. His body and clothing were stained reddish orange from the clay. We patted him on the back and cheered loudly. Slowly, Jimmy stood up and, with both fists clenched, raised his arms in the air. He looked to the sky. His face showed both relief and exhilaration. On that day for Jimmy, one instinct - the determination to achieve - had overcome another instinct - fear.

If determination was success, Jimmy had it in spades. He needed this force of character to persevere through the trials that he faced in his early life. It sustained him through thick and thin.

Later in life, Jimmy suffered much loss. He lost his father and his mother. He lost his room at the "little house." He lost his routine and his security. It had to be disconcerting for Jimmy. No one knows exactly how he felt deep down. Was it devastation, loss, grief, fear or loneliness? Was it all of these emotions and more besides? His family and loved ones tried to help as they could. There must have been times though, when the only things Jimmy had were his faith, perhaps a memory of his love for life, and his determination.

In many ways at this time of his life, if not before, Jimmy had become his own man.

CHAPTER TWENTY-SIX
HIS BIRTHDAY

Jimmy's birthdays were sizable. His parties were not necessarily crowded soirees. Some of his parties were large family gatherings. Others were very small, private affairs. Jimmy's birthdays were sizable because they were so long. Their length seemed to grow year by year.

Jimmy didn't just have a birth *day*. Jimmy had a birth *season*. And as self-described "shy" as Jimmy was, he was a key proponent of extending the season. Jimmy was born on October 22. A person, however, could be visiting Alabama in July, and Jimmy would decide he needed something.

"Jimmy, do you want me to take you shopping?"

"*You doe 'head.*"

"Would you like me to buy something for you, Jimmy?"

"*My birfday.*"

One year Uncle Mark calculated that Jimmy received his first "birthday present" in April and his last one in December. That year, his birthday season extended from April until December.

Jimmy's expectations for his birthday grew throughout his life. One year there was a large family celebration in Alabama on his birthday. Jimmy's birthday was on a Tuesday. It was a major event and he received an abundance of presents.

On the following Friday, a package came in the mail. Getting the mail was Jimmy's job. He walked into the house holding the package up for all to see, confident that yet another present had arrived for him. As it turned out, the package was actually for Grandmother, not him. The storm clouds rolled in over that injustice. Jimmy moped for hours.

Jimmy loved to spend the night at his brother's houses for birthday parties. He got to eat a meal of his choosing, followed by cake and ice cream. Jimmy was a big fan of cake and ice cream. He also was a big fan of the birthday presents that followed.

After the presents came games. One of Jimmy's favorite birthday games was hide and seek. Jimmy hid and the other party goers would seek. Jimmy preference was for the primary seeker to be a pretty niece such as Laurie, Kay, or Rachel. Jimmy selected a hiding place as the "seeker" counted loudly. Jimmy's chortles and snickers betrayed his "hiding place" in short order. When Jimmy was "found," then the niece needed to *"tittlee hair."* "Tittlee hair" was a rather unusual ritual whereby the hider would have his head and hair tickled by the seeker. It may have been unusual, but it was a necessary part of the birthday game of "hide and seek."

Members of the Martin family still had a lot of contact with Jimmy when he was at Rainbow Omega. His brothers and sisters made frequent telephone calls to him. They visited him regularly. The family also picked him up and took him to their homes for visits and for special occasions - birthdays (especially, his birthday) and, of course, Thanksgiving.

A number of years before, when he was living with Papa and Meme, Jimmy demonstratively hated to see people leave. It occurred to me then that Jimmy's everyday life might not be that exciting. He probably experienced periods of boredom. I resolved to contact him at least once a week. I called him, wrote him letters, mailed him postcards, or acquired some type of souvenir to send to him as often as I could.

After Jimmy went to Rainbow, I still tried to call him. I didn't call him as much as Sharon though. Sharon picked up the mantle of communication with Jimmy. She called him at least once a week. The content of the telephone calls became a routine, a routine that was reassuring to Jimmy - especially when he first lived at Rainbow. Sharon remembers the content of those early calls:

Rainbow House Manager: "Jimmy…phone for you …"
Jimmy: *H'llo???*
Sharon: Hi, Jimmy, it's Sharon.
J: *SHARON!! That you, Sharon?*
S: Yes, sweetheart, it's me, Sharon.
J: *Wanna tell you sumptin … yeah lub you.*
S: Thank you, honey, I love you, too.
J: *You lub me? You sure-sure?*
S: Yes, Jimmy, I love you so-oo much.
J: *Sharon … wanna ast you sumptin … why you tie me up wif rope?*
S: Well, Jimmy, you were really sad and hurting and you said you were going to run away, so I had to tie you up with rope…
J: *Hmmmph … why you tie me up wif rope?*
S: Because you were going to run away … and we need you, you are part of our family, and our hearts would hurt so much if we didn't have our Jimmy…
J: *You thad me run 'way?*
S: Oh, yes, sweetheart, I couldn't let you run away because you are too special and important to us. We need you, and we love you too much to let you run away.
J: [Giggling] *Hmm … feel lite Samson … why you tie me up wif rope?*
S: You tell me, honey … why did I tie you up with rope?
J: *Sharon … wanna tell you sumptin … you weady?*
S: Yes, sweetheart, tell me.
J: [Repeated kissy-smacking noises] *Uummm, mmmm, kissy smack, kissy smack.*
S: Thank you, Jimmy, I love you, too.

J: [Pause] *Your turn!*

S: Okay, Jimmy, you ready?

J: *Weal weady!*

S: [Big kissy - smack sound!]

J: *More?*

S: Yes, honey, lots more, I love you sooo much.

J: *Yeah doe 'head!*

S: [Big kissy - smack sound!]

J: *You tum see me?*

S: Yes, sweetie, I'll be coming to see you. I sure do miss you!

J: *Ah, ha! You want me tum see you?*

S: I'd love for you to come to North Carolina sometime to see me. We'll have to wait to see...

J: *You want me tum lib wif you?*

S: Well, Jimmy, I sure want you to come see me sometime. I hear that you have a job and you get paper money. You need to work hard to save your paper money so you can come see me sometime.

J: *Hmmph! Jan pick wrong one. I tum lib wif YOU!* [His row leader, Jan, committed the unpardonable sin of being an Alabama fan!]

J: *Sharon, wanna tell you sumptin...* [Lowers voice to whisper with urgency]... *Dunno why he don lite me. No lite fight. No lite hit. Hurt my heart. Lord no lite fight. You know why he don lite me?* [Note: Could it be because Jimmy bit him last week?]

S: Well, sweetheart, you're right ... the Lord doesn't want us to fight.

J: *No lite talk about it ... Sharon ... wanna ast you sumptin ... why you tie me up wif rope?*

S: Well, Jimmy, you were really sad and hurting and you said you were going to run away, so I had to tie you up with rope...

J: *Hmmmph...why you tie me up wif rope?*

S: Because you were going to run away… and we need you, you are part of our family, and our hearts would hurt so much if we didn't have our Jimmy…

J: *You thad me run 'way?*

S: Oh, yes, sweetheart, I couldn't let you run away because you are too special and important to us. We need you, and we love you too much to let you run away

J: [Giggling] *Hmm…feel lite Samson…why you tie me up wif rope?*

S: You tell me, honey … why did I tie you up with rope?

J: *Sharon…wanna tell you sumptin…you ready?*

S: Yes, sweetheart, tell me

J: [Repeated kissy-smacking noises] *Uummm, mmmm, kissy smack, kissy smack.*

S: Thank you, Jimmy, I love you, too.

J: [Pause] *Your turn!*

S: Okay, Jimmy, you ready?

J: *Weal weady!*

S: [Big kissy - smack sound!]

J: *More?*

S: Yes, honey, lots more, I love you sooo much.

J: *Yeah doe 'head!*

S: [Big kissy - smack sound!]

J: *My mudder…my fadder, up in heben. Got 2 mudder…2 fadder…*[Long silence]…*no feel lite talk about it…make you thad. No lite make you thad.*

S: Okay, honey, let's talk about something happy. I know somebody who's going to have a birthday soon.

J: *Hmmm…might be me! You want me tum your houth my birfday?*

S: Jimmy, that would be soo much fun! Maybe you can come have your birthday in North Carolina sometime.

J: *You want me tum lib wif you? No lite Rainbow. I tum lib wif you!*

S: Honey, I'm not sure about that...

J: *Me talk Mike. You ast Mike me tum lib wif you.*

S: Well, I know Mike is going to bring me to see you on Big Turkey Day.

J: *You tum Bid Turtey Day? You sit by me Bid Turtey Day?*

S: Yes, Jimmy, we're coming Big Turkey Day, and, oh, yes, I want to sit by you Big Turkey Day. You don't let anybody else tease you and sit by you because I want to sit by you Big Turkey Day! There will be a lot of our family there...let's think about everybody who will be there Big Turkey Day...

J: *Lotsa lotsa people dere...feel sorry Betty Hubbard. She no know me, me no know her!*

S: Yes, but think about all the people who will be there who love you soo much...

J: *Sharon...wanna ast you sumptin...why you tie me up wif rope?*

S: Well, Jimmy, you were really sad and hurting and you said you were going to run away, so I had to tie you up with rope...

J: *Hmmmph...why you tie me up wif rope?*

S: Because you were going to run away...and we need you, you are part of our family, and our hearts would hurt so much if we didn't have our Jimmy...

J: *You thad me run 'way?*

S: Oh, yes, sweetheart, I couldn't let you run away because you are too special and important to us. We need you, and we love you too much to let you run away

J: [Giggling) *Hmm...feel lite Samson...why you tie me up wif rope?*

S: You tell me, honey ... why did I tie you up with rope?

J: *Sharon...wanna tell you sumptin...you ready?*

S: Yes, sweetheart, tell me.

J: [Repeated kissy-smacking noises] *Uummm, mmmm, kissy smack, kissy smack.*

S: Thank you, Jimmy, I love you, too.

J: [Pause] *Your turn!*

S: Okay, Jimmy, you ready?

J: *Weal weady!*

S: [Big kissy - smack!]

J: *More?*

S: Yes, honey, lots more, I love you sooo much.

J: *Yeah doe 'head!*

S: [Note: Whoever answered the phone at Rainbow usually asked that Sharon encourage Jimmy either to do or to refrain from doing something.] Jimmy, I want you to do something for me. Will you do something for me?

J: *Yeah lite.*

S: Sweetheart, I want you to be real nice to _____. He is there to help you. I want you to let him help you.

J: *Hmmph! No lite Rainbow! Me tum lib wif you!*

S: But will you do that for me? Will you be nice?

J: [With passionate feeling!] *You tell Mike me tum lib wif YOU!*

S: Well, we will come see you soon.

J: *Sharon, wanna tell you sumptin...* [Whispers] *...I lub you, honey...*

S: I love you so much! You are soo special! There is a special place in my heart that only my Jimmy can fill. You are just who God wanted me to have to be my special Uncle Jimmy...

[Jimmy's appreciative "ummm – hmmmm's" and "ah-ha's" punctuate what Sharon was saying until they are eventually heard from a distance because Jimmy has set the phone down.]

J: [From a distance as Jimmy seeks assistance in hanging up the phone.] *Sumbahdy! Hey, sumbaaaaaaaahdy!*

As Jimmy expressed to Sharon on a weekly basis, he had long dreamed of visiting North Carolina and celebrating his birthday there. In October of 2002, Uncle Tim helped make this dream a reality and facilitated a grand birthday event for Jimmy. Tim picked Jimmy up from Rainbow and made the long drive with Jimmy to Uncle Mark's house near Asheville, North Carolina. At Uncle Mark's, they had his first birthday party and spent the night.

Uncle Mark and Uncle Tim then drove Jimmy to Sharon's house in Durham, North Carolina. The next day, Sharon and Mike took Jimmy to Sharon's alma mater, the University of North Carolina at Chapel Hill. There Jimmy agreeably posed for videos and a series of pictures at famous campus landmarks like the Old Well. He posed as a college student, a football player, and a sports fan (*"Want Tar Heel beat Tide"*). Jimmy attracted numerous stares from curious students passing by, and he waved at the pretty coed's. They must have wondered "What type of photo shoot is that?"

The following day family came from all over the region for a large second birthday celebration. My family came from Charlotte; my brother, Daniel, came from Asheville; my mother, Rachel, from Virginia; and Joseph (Uncle Daniel's son) came from Elizabethton, TN where he was attending the Moody Bible Institute aviation school. Even my friend, Brian Ascher, who lived in Durham, came.

We lavished Jimmy with presents and attention. One present we found for Jimmy was a Mattel "Classic Football game," a hand held electronic football game with beeps, whistles and lights. Jimmy had this game in the 1970's and he played it for hours on end. When Jimmy opened the present, he recognized the game and immediately began playing it.

No present, however, was treasured any more than an Auburn cap signed by the head coach of the Auburn Tigers himself that read:

To Jimmy
War Eagle
Tommy Tuberville

Jimmy quickly put the hat on his head. He stood up and saluted. Then he tipped his cap to the assembled guests, proclaiming *"Tauburn numma one!"*

Accompanying the Auburn hat was a letter to Jimmy from Coach Tuberville himself, and an award from the Auburn athletic department that read:

Presented to James Carlton Stuckey
Loyal All-American War Eagle Fan of the Auburn Tigers

From Durham, Uncle Mark and Uncle Tim took Jimmy to Rachel's house in Virginia. Yet a third birthday party was held there. They had the usual commotion that surrounded Jimmy when Jimmy ignited a fire by discarding wrapping paper from a present onto a nearby candle.

Going to see the "Carolina people" had always been a dream of Jimmy's. He had talked about it for a long time. His family worked and made the dream a reality during that year's birthday season.

CHAPTER TWENTY-SEVEN
JUBILEE

Jimmy had always been apprehensive of death. He didn't like to discuss death or even to think about the prospect of dying. Jimmy loved life. He enjoyed people and he enjoyed interacting with them. He loved laughter and he loved to have fun. Jimmy was grateful for life. Discussions about death bothered Jimmy. If a conversation touched on death or if Jimmy heard about some one else who died, he said, *"Tant you, Jesus! No me die! Feel 'live!"*

In the months following his Carolina birthday trip, Jimmy's dementia slowly increased. He began to have lapses where he could not remember names of friends. The dementia grew to the point he sometimes did not recognize family members. These lapses became more frequent until they became the norm.

Occasionally an occurrence would spark Jimmy's memory. In May of 2004, Uncle Daniel was asked to speak at a fundraiser for Rainbow Omega. Many members of the Martin family attended as well as James Edge and "Big Jimmy" - Jimmy Glenn. Jimmy was also there. Uncle Daniel lovingly shared about Jimmy's background and family.

Uncle Tim says:

At the fundraiser for Rainbow Omega, Jimmy was not aware enough of his surroundings even to eat without help. After the fundraiser though, "Big Jimmy" came to "Little Jimmy's" table and started singing "Deep and Wide." Jimmy joined in the singing and even did some of the hand motions to the song. It was amazing to see how much this song stimulated his mind.

During his time of dementia, singing this song was the best way to see some sense of recognition in Jimmy's eyes.

By Thanksgiving, 2004 though, Jimmy recognized only a few people. A voice or a face might jolt his memory. One minute he called a person by name and the next minute he might ask the very same person *"What your name?"*

Jimmy's formerly confident stride became a hesitant shuffle. He was unsure of his balance and of his step. Jimmy required assistance everywhere he went.

Jimmy's care at Rainbow continued, and it increased in proportion to his needs. In late summer, 2005, Jimmy aspirated some food. He was taken to the hospital, but developed pneumonia. The uncles provided constant care, and Rachel and Uncle Mark drove down and stayed in the hospital with Jimmy for a week. He slowly improved.

While Jimmy was in the hospital, the doctors found some bleeding in his brain. The family dared to hope. Maybe surgery would not only correct the bleeding problem, but maybe it would also help reverse Jimmy's mental deterioration. After the surgery though, Jimmy's mental condition only improved marginally.

Jimmy went back to Rainbow for a brief time. He had a relapse of the pneumonia, however, and returned to the hospital. Uncle Tim, Uncle Stephen, Uncle Daniel, and Uncle Thomas gave him 24 hour care. Other family members and members of Jimmy's Rainbow family visited him, but there was not anything anyone could do. Jimmy's condition slowly deteriorated until he slipped into a coma.

The coma lasted for a few days. The manner in which Jimmy died was a blessing. He did not have to experience the fear of impending death. As the pneumonia slowly constricted his breathing, Jimmy was not conscious so he did not realize what was happening.

Uncle Thomas says:

When Jimmy was in a coma, he had a lot of difficulty breathing. His body struggled for oxygen. With each breath, his back and

stomach muscles tensed and his face turned red. He was in a coma, but he was still fighting to stay alive.

Jimmy's body struggled for each breath until it finally could breathe no more. Jimmy died with his brothers, Tim and Thomas, beside him along with his Rainbow "brother," Wayne and Wayne's wife, Darlene. Uncle Daniel had just left the hospital a few minutes earlier to go back to the motel to rest, but could not get back to the hospital before Jimmy passed away.

Wayne says:

My wife, Darlene, and I were driving home from the hospital that evening after Jimmy had died. We were talking about Jimmy's new home and how he must be seeing things now that he had never seen before. At that moment, we saw a shooting star in the sky. Darlene looked at me and said "There goes Jimmy!"

Jimmy's funeral was attended by hundreds of people. The viewing and reception were held immediately before the funeral. In attendance were family members, van loads of residents from Rainbow Omega, and friends and persons who had known Jimmy throughout his life.

In the viewing room were tables loaded with memorabilia and items that Jimmy liked to keep in his room - an Auburn shirt and plaque; Jimmy's camera and some pictures; and Jimmy's "diploma" - the educational award he had received for "Diligence in Learning." There were videotapes of family gatherings taken by Aunt Loretta. Sharon brought a collage of pictures from Jimmy's North Carolina birthday trip. One of the most prized possessions was a framed picture of Jimmy with Papa and Meme.

Jimmy's casket was surrounded by flowers sent by friends and family. One floral arrangement close to his casket was from Rainbow

Omega. It had multiple rosebuds - one for each resident who lived at Rainbow.

During the reception, both crying and laughter could be heard. Crying was heard as friends and family said goodbye to a beloved brother, uncle and friend. Laughter was heard as those present recounted Jimmy's life, his manner, and, of course, stories about Jimmy. Often, the crying and laughter occurred simultaneously. Even when a loved one was grieving, a memory of Jimmy, or the thought of the expressions he would use, couldn't help but bring a smile to the lips.

A number of people spoke at Jimmy's funeral - first, Stentson Carpenter (Chairman and Founder of Rainbow Omega), and then Wayne, Jimmy's house manager and friend. They shared about the vision for Rainbow and what Jimmy's time there had meant to the Rainbow community.

Jimmy Glenn, who had introduced Jimmy to the Martin family, shared about Jimmy's early life. He led the assembly in singing *"Deep and Wide"* (with accompanying hand motions).

Sharon and I both shared. Sharon told of Jimmy's love. Through her tears, she spoke of the emotional tenderness that Jimmy demonstrated to her and to others during his whole life.

I was honored to share the impact of Jimmy on my own life. Each of us may remember a few people that we have met, but we don't meet many people that are remarkable. Jimmy, however, was both memorable and remarkable. When people met Jimmy, they remembered him. And those people were changed as well. Jimmy changed their perspective - their perspective on disability; their perspective on life; and their perspective on humanity. Jimmy was an extremely influential person.

Jimmy's character taught us valuable lessons:

1. Life has value. Jimmy's life proved that a handicap does not have to diminish the joy or quality of a person's life. Life has value, so value the lives of others. Look for talents and gifts that God has given each soul - whether that soul appears great or small.

2. Know who you are. Jimmy refused to allow his spirit to be subdued by the problems presented by his condition. Know who you are, but realize that you will not be who you were created to be until you find and fulfill God's purpose for your life. Jimmy's life had a purpose. He was the treasure of his family - the crowning jewel of Papa and Meme's vision.

3. Love counts most. Jimmy was the recipient of uncommon love. In return, he shared that love with all around him. Love counts most, so endeavor to grow in love.

Finally, Uncle Daniel, who officiated the service as pastor, spoke. He told of Jimmy's love of the Lord Jesus, and how that love had filled Jimmy's heart throughout his life in both joyful and difficult times. Jimmy used to say, "Lord Jesus live in my heart." Uncle Daniel then shared the simple gospel of the Lord Jesus Christ. Christ died for us – the just for the unjust, that we might be reconciled to God and have eternal life with Him.

I was honored to be chosen as a pallbearer for Jimmy along with my uncles. It was an honor to me because of who Jimmy was. It was also an honor because of who my uncles were. They had sacrificed and given unselfishly of themselves for years in order to provide for Jimmy. They did not allow Papa and Meme's vision for family to die with Papa and Meme. As they sadly carried their brother's body to his grave to lay it to rest, they could truthfully affirm that they had fulfilled Meme's dying request to "Take care of Jimmy."

Jimmy was buried in Brookside Memorial Gardens in Millbrook, Alabama. His grave was located beside the graves of Papa and Meme. Uncle Daniel said a few words at the graveside service and we prayed. As family and friends were leaving the cemetery, we saw a Rainbow resident who was standing near Jimmy's casket looking at it. He was alone without anyone around him. Tears were streaming down his cheeks. His arm was raised and he was waving goodbye to Jimmy.

Jimmy died on September 15, 2005. It had been exactly 50 years since Jimmy had come to live with the Martin family.

Jubilee had come.

> Born James Carlton Stuckey Jr. on October 22, 1949, Jimmy passed from this life to be with his Lord and Savior on September 15, 2005, following a short illness. Jimmy was integrated into the family of the late Thomas and Agnes Martin of Wetumpka, AL when they assumed care of him in September 1955, and has been a vital and beloved member of their family since then. Jimmy's condition of Down's Syndrome in no way limited his capacity for love and communication. Known for his pithy sayings and descriptive vocabulary, his enthusiasm and fervent spirit enriched the lives of all who knew him. From "Make my heart happy" to "Gods knows" to fierce Auburn loyalty, Jimmy expressed himself wholeheartedly. Jimmy often affirmed his faith and told friend and stranger alike that "Jesus lives in my heart.... The Lord is my shepherd.... Love never fails." The "spice and sparkle" he brought to his family was shared with his friends at Rainbow Omega in Eastaboga, AL where he lived in recent years.

POSTLOGUE

We were sitting at the breakfast table in Alabama at the house of my Grandmother and Grandaddy. This was one of my favorite places and one of my favorite times. We had just finished a wonderful Meme breakfast. We were sitting there - Grandaddy, Grandmother, Jimmy and my family.

I looked across the table and saw my Grandfather - almost bald up top with tufts of gray hair on the sides and back of his head surrounding the bald middle. He was elderly, but wiry and in great shape. He had a distinct nose and clear eyes.

I saw my Grandmother - kindness radiating from her eyes. Her silvery white hair was pinned in a bun at the top of her head. She had lost some teeth over the years and had a snaggle-toothed smile. Yet that smile was one of the most pleasant ones I have ever seen, and she shared it often.

As I looked at my grandparents and thought of their years and of their lives, I imagined that vast wisdom must be stored in their hearts and minds. I turned to Grandaddy and said, "Grandaddy, if you could tell us anything, what would that be?"

I had opened the door and I waited expectantly. This question was actually a brave one. Grandaddy could talk awhile. He usually let Meme carry social conversation. But if Grandaddy got focused on a topic of interest to him, he could talk for hours. But I asked the question. I braced myself for what could be a long lecture or a list of life instructions.

Grandaddy paused for a minute. He took a breath and looked me squarely in the eyes. He said three words – "Love one another."

Grandaddy paused again. Silence filled the room. Every eye at that table was focused on him. We waited to see what else he would say. But he had no elaboration. Slowly and deliberately, he repeated, "Love...one...another."

Other Books by David Thurman:

THE CALL Book One – Functional
Keys to Effective Discipleship

THE CALL Book Two – Foundational
Progressive Fivefold Function

THE CALL Book Three – Fruitful
Transforming Your Community

Available on Amazon.com and other online stores